Restored

"In this wonderfully comforting guide for dealing with abuse, Dr. Woodard gently leads the abused through a process of Scriptural healing. This book is on such a relevant subject and in great need not only in our society but in our churches, as well. It is a great tool for both the abused and the counsellor."

—Wendyjo S. Householder
Hope4TheHurting.org
Widow / Mother / Missionary with Reformers Unanimous / Counselor to hurting women

"When Don Woodard writes of the hope one can find after abuse, he writes from the expansive ministry experience as a pastor and church leader. Woodard is no theorist; he has more than thirty years of practical, successful experience in counseling those who have been abused, leading them to a close, personal walk with the Saviour, and hope for a new life free from past abuses. I am a personal witness to his success and his own walk having known him and witnessed his life and ministry since he was young teen. I am excited and pleased to know that as you read, you will discover the simple, biblical truths that can transform an abused life and give the freedom from its weight of guilt and oppression."

—Michael A. Hand, Ph.D.
Partnership Mission Strategist
Oklahoma City, OK

"*Restored: Living and Loving after Abuse* has not only opened my eyes to "letting go and letting God." It's also allowed me the opportunity to refresh my heart and strengthen my faith in HIM. In this biblical based self help guide Dr. Woodard has given us an abundance of encouraging truth powered by Scripture for anyone that has struggled or continues to struggle with any form of abuse. The counsel given in this book provides us with a lifetime resource of hope, peace and life."

—Heather F.
Abuse victim, now victor

"This book has been what I needed, I didn't know it at the time, I knew I needed help but to live and love again, it wasn't possible, so I thought. As I started helping out with this book and telling how I felt on things or how I saw things, it began to change me, a transformation was taking place. I found hope, I began to feel at peace and I began to like myself again, I am beginning to see that I can live and love again."

—J.L.
Mother /Abuse Survivor

"Through the many years of ministry Dr. Don Woodard has realized there are too many lives that have been affected by abuse of some kind and that as a people we are crying out for help. Dr. Don has proven his heart for helping the hurting again in *Restored: Living and Loving after Abuse*."

—Melissa Davis
Wife / Mother / Christian Counselor / Gospel Singer / Abuse Survivor

"Dr. Don Woodard's book will touch and change hearts both of victims of abuse and those who minister love to them. The love of Jesus Christ rises from the pages to lift the hurting and ravaged to newness of life."

—Dr. Ernie Moore
Retired Pastor / Missions Director / Author

"My good friend Don Woodard has a heart for the Lord and a heart for people, hurting people in particular. Jesus said he came to heal the brokenhearted, today we have hurting people everywhere. People whose lives have been affected by somebody else's sin, this book will help those victims to begin to heal and discover new joy in life that can be found only in Christ."

—Pastor Matt Swiatkowski
Kearny, New Jersey

"As an evangelist, there's hardly a church where I preach for more than a day where I do not meet someone who has suffered for years or decades after being abused. This book will help them or help you help them to get victory over defeat, depression, and broken relationships."

—Dr. Bruce Miller
Evangelist / Founder of Atlantic Coast Baptist
College Laurel, Delaware

"Daily I endeavor to help teenage girls who have suffered inconceivable circumstances leaving them feeling worthless and hopeless. *Restored: Living and Loving after Abuse* is a gift from God. Using the Word of God, Dr. Woodard, compassionately guides the broken to a victorious life of hope, love, and happiness through Jesus Christ."

—Lori Harvey
Missionary with Farmer Christian Girls Home & Academy

"In his book *Restored: Living and Loving after Abuse*, Dr. Don Woodard has woven a tapestry of love, forgiveness, hope and healing. His skillful use of powerful Scripture, loving and compassionate insight will lead the reader on a journey of self discovery and awareness of the power of love. This book is a must read for anyone who has suffered abuse of has someone in their life that has. I urge you to read this wonderfully written book and discover the life God has richly planned for you, full of love and beauty."

—Tonda Tayloy-Bently

Restored
Living and Loving After Abuse

Dr. Don Woodard

AMBASSADOR INTERNATIONAL
GREENVILLE, SOUTH CAROLINA & BELFAST, NORTHERN IRELAND

www.ambassador-international.com

Restored
Living and Loving After Abuse
© 2018 by Dr. Don Woodard
All rights reserved

ISBN: 978-1-62020-259-3
eISBN: 978-1-62020-359-0

Disclaimer

The author of this book is a biblical counselor. This book contains scriptural principles for ministering to people who have suffered physical, emotional, and sexual abuse. It is not intended to replace pastoral or other counseling practices.

All word definitions are from The Webster's 1828 Dictionary

Unless indicated otherwise, Scripture quotations are taken from the King James Version, The Authorized Version. Public Domain.

Cover Design & Typesetting by Hannah Nichols

AMBASSADOR INTERNATIONAL
Emerald House
411 University Ridge, Suite B14
Greenville, SC 29601, USA
www.ambassador-international.com

AMBASSADOR BOOKS
The Mount
2 Woodstock Link
Belfast, BT6 8DD, Northern Ireland, UK
www.ambassadormedia.co.uk

The colophon is a trademark of Ambassador

For Sara

CONTENTS

ACKNOWLEDGMENTS 11

INTRODUCTION 13

CHAPTER ONE
SOMEBODY DOES LOVE YOU 15

CHAPTER TWO
A NEW JOURNEY 21

CHAPTER THREE
TAKING BACK MY LIFE 25

CHAPTER FOUR
PAST-PRESENT-FUTURE: WHAT I CAN CHANGE 33

CHAPTER FIVE
THE POWER OF FORGIVENESS 47

CHAPTER SIX
QUESTIONS FROM THE HEART, ANSWERS FROM GOD 59

CHAPTER SEVEN
TRUST 73

CHAPTER EIGHT
CONFRONTING GIANTS 83

CHAPTER NINE
PREPARE FOR WARFARE 93

CHAPTER TEN
SELF-VALUE 101

CHAPTER ELEVEN
WRITTEN ON YOUR HEART 109

CHAPTER TWELVE
POUR OUT YOUR HEART 115

CHAPTER THIRTEEN
HOPE 121

CHAPTER FOURTEEN
PERSONAL PEACE 129

CHAPTER FIFTEEN
BEAUTY FOR ASHES 139

A LETTER TO MY READERS 147

TESTIMONIES 149

LIVING AND POWERFUL WORDS 161

ABOUT THE AUTHOR 171

ACKNOWLEDGMENTS

This project would not have been possible without the help of my amazing team. (Some requested that their full name not be used).

Melissa Davis, J.L.H., Suzi F., Pastor Matt Swiatkowski, Darlene D., Sean Mulroney, and Doug. D.

And a special thank you to Patricia Longmire for her amazing work on editing the manuscript.

INTRODUCTION

I MET DR. DON WOODARD in January of 2000 while sitting with my son in a Youth Conference at a church in Palmer, Texas. Dr. Don was sharing with the teens how young men should treat young ladies with dignity. He spoke of men treating women with the utmost respect, in fact, his words were "guys treat them like fine china, you don't use fine china carelessly, and you take special care of it and treat it very special every time you take it out, like a treasure, not like a toy." I believe that was the first time in my life that I heard a man say women were fragile; treat them with care and respect. It felt wonderful to know some man I had never seen before was talking about how to respect ladies. I was a recently single mom with three children and had never had that kind of love or respect in my marriage. Surely, he was talking about the teen girls there that day and not to a woman like me. The more I listened that day the more I realized he was talking about all women. I left that day wishing someone had told me earlier in my life that God loved me no matter where I was or what had happened.

Dr. Woodard has been in the Ministry for over 30 years, in those years he has opened an orphanage in Haiti, served as an evangelist and pastor, authored books, and counseled hundreds if not thousands of men, women, teens, and children. Through the many years of ministry, he has realized there are too many lives that have been affected by abuse of some kind and that as a people we are crying out for help. Dr. Don has proven his heart for helping those who are hurting in *Restored: Living and Loving after Abuse*.

He shows us how God can renew our heart and our mind by teaching us to trust Him and let go of our past. He shows us through Christ's teachings that forgiveness is for us to take back the power of our lives that was taken from us by evil-doers. He shows us how we can become new in Christ and how Christ can write a new story on the tablets of our heart. He walks us through the right way to face our giants and become fearless warriors as we take our lives back.

It's time to allow God to rewrite our heart story. It's time to give our hearts a good cleaning and turn the pen over to one who will write with love and compassion. The words spoken to us can be found in God's Word, and those words are words of love, peace, comfort, and promises by God Himself. We learn how to face the giants in our life and how to overcome them just as David overcame Goliath.

Offer God your heart, and He will deliver a new love to you and write His love upon your heart. He will heal you and use your life in a way that will glorify and magnify our Lord Jesus Christ. Jesus Christ loves you and is waiting with open arms for you to come to Him. He loves you with no strings attached.

2 Corinthians 5:17 *"Therefore if any man be in Christ, he is a new creature: old things are passed away; behold all things are become new."*

Melissa McCarty Davis

CHAPTER ONE
SOMEBODY DOES LOVE YOU

THE GREATEST OF ALL HUMAN needs is the need to be loved. To know for certain without any doubt that we are loved. The challenge for every abused person that I have ever counseled is the lack of confidence in knowing that they are truly loved, followed by not believing that they could ever be loved. The feeling of not being loved is, in my view, the worst of all experiences in life because our assurances that we are loved, come from self-value and hope. Over the years, I have talked with people that have experienced physical and emotional abuse so severely that they found an embrace, which was intended to be an innocent expression of affection, to be painful. Even to be touched physically hurt them. Just as there are expressions that confirm to us that we are loved there are also expressions and actions that confirm that we are not loved.

In the Bible, we can find examples of people who may have questioned if anyone really loved them. The Samaritan woman at the well would have doubted that anyone loved her, yet Jesus came to her to personally express His love to her (John 4:1-38). The man that lived in the tombs probably didn't believe anyone loved him either, but Jesus came to him and cast out the demons and made him whole (Mark 5:1-20). The leper whom no one would even touch because of his leprosy would not have felt loved, but Jesus came to him and touched him and made him whole (Mark 1:40-41).

Like numerous others who have experienced abuse, you probably struggle with believing you are loved. It is my sole desire to convince you of one certain truth, somebody does love you! No matter what your past is like, somebody does love you! No matter where you came from, somebody does love you! No matter what others have told you, somebody does love you! No matter what your family circumstances are, somebody does love you! No matter what you think of yourself, somebody does love you! And no matter if you believe it or not, somebody does love you!

I LOVE YOU

I love you. Because I know there is a God in Heaven that loves me unconditionally, I'm able to love you. Because of God's love I'm able to love you as a fellow human being that Jesus Christ loves and as a human being that has experienced disappointment and hurt in your life. I love you! Because I believe that if given the means to overcome and make the most of your life, you would. Because my heart hurts at the idea of you not believing or even knowing that someone somewhere loves you, I love you! You may not know me, and I may not know you, we may or may not be related, but because God has blessed me beyond my own understanding, I want you to know that I love you!

OTHERS LOVE YOU

I know there are others that love you, some of them may not know how to express it, but they love you. There are people who have suffered some of the same hurts you have suffered and because they can relate to your struggles, they know the fears, challenges, and heartaches you have experienced, they love you! There are Christian people that know the love of God and love you because you are someone God created for the purpose of being loved. They love Jesus Christ and so they love you too! These are the people that cheer for you; they want you to win. They want you to have confidence, to rise up, and to be victorious. And above all things they want you to know that somebody does love you, and they want you to know that Jesus Christ loves you!

JESUS LOVES YOU

The greatest truth in the world is revealed in a children's song, "Jesus Loves Me." The first verse says, "Jesus loves me—this I know, for the Bible tells me so; little ones to him belong, —they are weak, but he is strong." What a blessing this truth is to my soul; I am weak, but He still loves me. The love of Jesus Christ is undeserved, unconditional, uncompromising, unwavering, immeasurable, empowering, sacrificial, and eternal. I could use even more adjectives to describe His love but there is not enough paper.

Jesus Christ loves you and me more than we could possibly imagine. He has proven His love in the most sacrificial way imaginable; He gave all of Himself. He loves us just as we are, and yet He desires to do a great work in our lives. He sees in us all that we can become. Here are a few things the Bible says about God's love for you:

"For God so loved the world (YOU), that he gave his only begotten Son, that whosoever believeth in him should not perish, but have everlasting life" (John 3:16).

"But God commendeth (committed) his love toward us, in that, while we were yet sinners, Christ died for us" (Romans 5:8).

"But God, who is rich in mercy, for his great love wherewith he loved us" (Ephesians 2:4).

"Now our Lord Jesus Christ himself, and God, even our Father, which hath loved us, and hath given us everlasting consolation and good hope through grace, Comfort your hearts, and stablish you in every good word and work" (2 Thessalonians 2:16-17).

"Herein is love, not that we loved God, but that he loved us, and sent his Son to be the propitiation (atoning sacrifice) for our sins" (1 John 4:10).

I can tell you that Jesus Christ loves you, and you may struggle to believe me because it is me telling you, someone you don't even know personally. But my friend, will you believe Jesus? Will you trust His expressions of love? Will you believe that Jesus Christ loves you unconditionally just as you are? Will you believe that His love for you has with it a desire for a relationship with you? Will you embrace His love and will you embrace Him as well? Will you receive His love, and will you love Him in return?

This book will be of little help to you if you do not have a personal relationship with Jesus Christ. Healing begins with faith in Him, and healing begins with a personal relationship with Him. Receiving the gift of love and eternal life in Jesus Christ is the beginning of victory.

A PERSONAL RELATIONSHIP WITH JESUS CHRIST

We need Jesus Christ because we are in a fallen state. We were born in a sinful, cursed world, we were born with a sin nature, and we have done wrong ourselves. Romans 5:8 says, *"But God commendeth (committed) his love toward us, in that, while we were yet sinners, Christ died for us."* Despite any wrong we have done, in spite of what we might think of our own lives, Jesus Christ loves us, and knowing we were sinners, He died on the Cross to pay the penalty of our sin. He shed His innocent blood to purchase our forgiveness.

ETERNAL LIFE IS A GIFT

The gift of God is eternal life. Romans 6:23 says, *"The wages (payment) of sin is death; but the gift of God is eternal life through Jesus Christ our Lord."* Eventually there is a time to pay and a time to be paid. Everyone will die, death is separation from life and for those who reject Jesus Christ death is separation from God forever in a place called Hell. The Bible describes Hell as a place of flames, torment, and agony. But God in His merciful and unconditional love offers a gift to us, the gift of eternal life in the presence of God in Heaven forever. The gift of eternal life is not something that we can earn, it's not something we can receive by being good, we can't purchase it, and we can't reach some level of spiritual perfection to obtain it. Eternal life in Jesus Christ is a gift that we must receive by faith.

ETERNAL LIFE IS RECEIVED BY FAITH

The Bible says in Romans 10:9-10,

That if thou shalt confess with thy mouth the Lord Jesus, and shalt believe in thine heart that God hath raised him from the dead, thou shalt be saved. For with the heart man believeth unto righteousness; and with the mouth confession is made unto salvation.

To confess means to agree. To receive the gift of eternal life, we must agree that we need God; we must agree that we have sinned against Him and that we need His forgiveness. His forgiveness is made possible by Jesus Christ going to the Cross and being raised back to life. It is not necessary that we understand everything, but it is necessary that we confess to Jesus Christ.

We must believe in our heart that God has raised him from the dead. *". . . For with the heart man believeth unto righteousness; and with the mouth confession is made unto salvation."* Everything we do in life is based on what we believe. What you believe about God and His Word is crucial. In order to receive the Gift of Eternal life, it is important that you believe Jesus Christ loves you, that He is the Son of God, that He was crucified on the Cross where He shed His blood and died for your sins. He paid the penalty of our sin in full. We must believe that three days after His death He arose from the dead victoriously over death, Hell, Satan, and Sin.

RECEIVE THE GIFT OF ETERNAL LIFE

Somebody does love you; His name if Jesus. He offers you eternal life and a relationship with Him. If you have never believed in Jesus Christ, if you have never confessed to Him, then I invite you to do so right now. Believe in your heart that He loves you and receive His gift of salvation. Believe and pray from your heart this model prayer. "God, I confess that I need Jesus Christ, I believe that He loves me and died for my sin. By faith I want to receive the gift of eternal life, I want to be forgiven, I want to have a personal relationship with Jesus, and I want to go to Heaven one day. Thank you for loving me and for forgiving me." Amen.

Dear friend, it is not the words that you prayed, but it is your faith in Jesus Christ that secures eternal life for you. If you just believed and received Jesus as your Saviour, let someone know.

CHAPTER TWO
A NEW JOURNEY

IN THE SUMMER OF 1994, I sat down on the front steps of a church next to a fifteen-year-old girl whom I will call Sara. One side of her head was shaved, and her remaining hair was dyed pink, which she let hang down in front of her face. Sara had cut marks on both of her arms and was dressed in black. The makeup around her eyes was dark, and she appeared emotionally distant. A lady in church brought Sara to hear me speak that night in a youth rally, and Sara asked afterwards if she could talk with me. As we sat on the steps that summer evening, Sara opened her heart up to me about the challenges she was facing in her life. She shared with me that she did not know who her father was and that her mother was currently in a lesbian relationship. Then with tears rolling down her cheeks and with her hands trembling, she told me things that I never imagined I would hear coming from a fifteen-year-old. Her mother's lesbian companion would go into Sara's room at night and climb in bed with her and take liberties. This of course was not the way Sara worded the behavior; I cleaned it up for publication. Before my conversation with Sara, I had heard of sexual abuse, and I was familiar with verbal and physical abuse, but this instance was only the second time anyone had ever described being sexually abused to me. A couple of years before this, a lady had revealed to me that her uncle, who raised her as a child, had abused her sexually as a young teenager.

My conversation with Sara began a new journey for me, a journey of searching for answers, hope, and healing for the future Sara's I would meet in life. In my conversation with Sara, I realized how serious a problem abuse is in the lives of thousands of people. Abuse is the taboo issue of our day. Abuse comes in all forms; it is in families, marriages, and in our churches of every brand and denomination. I have since learned that there are many Sara's and Stevens in the world that are looking for answers, looking for someone to care, to confirm that they have value, to love them, to assure them they can live and love again, and to offer them hope in their journey of life.

Viewing life as a journey is a positive way to approach the events we encounter and help deal with the struggles we've confronted on our journey. The word journey is defined as "a passage from one place to another." In our journey of life, we travel through places of darkness and places of light. We encounter people on this path that we can put in the categories of people of darkness and people of light.

From the darkness of their hearts, the abusers seek out their victims whom they can easily hurt physically, emotionally, and spiritually. Jesus Christ said to these kinds of people, *"Ye are of your father the devil, and the lusts of your father ye will do. He was a murderer from the beginning, and abode not in the truth, because there is no truth in him. When he speaketh a lie, he speaketh of his own: for he is a liar, and the father of it"* (John 8:44). I have met people of darkness, and I have counseled scores of people who have encountered people of darkness. They have been hurt deeply and abused in some of the worse ways imaginable. Some of these people of darkness were within their own families, neighborhoods, and, yes, even within their churches.

I have served in the ministry for over thirty years, and I am aware of the evil that has been committed against the innocent within the sanctity of the name of Christ. There is no excuse for any form of abuse, and when people are abused under the banner of Christ and His cause, He sees it as a grave offence. Jesus Christ said in Matthew 18:6, *"But whoso shall offend one of these little ones which believe in me, it were better for him that a millstone were hanged about his neck, and that he were drowned in the depth of the sea."*

I've also been acquainted with people of light, people that seek to shine forth the Light of God's love, truth, and peace. Jesus Christ told His followers, *"Let your light so shine before men, that they may see your good works, and glorify your Father which is in heaven."* In this world of darkness, God has bestowed us with light, the light of truth, hope, peace, love, and victory for our journey toward living and loving again.

The purpose of this book is to shine forth the light of biblical truth and hope for your life journey. We may not be able to address every aspect of your personal circumstances in this volume, but our prayer is that you will gain strength from the biblical principles you find in these pages—strength that will carry you in your journey from the place of despair to the place of hope, from the place of hurt to the place of healing, from the place of turmoil to the place of peace, and from a life of brokenness to a life of living and loving again. This book has been prayed over, written, and prepared for the Saras and Stevens of the world. That they may know they have great value, they are loved, there is hope, and they can live and love again. May God strengthen you as you embark on this journey, and may you find peace! God Loves You!

CHAPTER THREE
TAKING BACK MY LIFE

IMAGINE A LITTLE GIRL HOLDING her most cherished teddy bear. The tiny child loves the teddy bear and imagines it to be her companion. An adult, with no regard for the child's emotions or attachment to the teddy bear, comes along and rips it out of her fragile arms and runs off with the teddy bear only to carelessly discard it into the trash heap of life. The child is powerless to stop the adult, unable to protect the beloved teddy bear, and just as incapable to take the teddy bear back. She cries out. No one hears her. She hurts inside, but no one understands. She does not have the words to explain what has happened, and, in her heart, she doubts that anyone would believe her or even listen to her story. So, she weeps in silent fear that the monster who took her teddy bear will return and take something more from her.

Most likely you don't have to imagine this at all. Perhaps you are like the child with the teddy bear because someone with no regard for your feelings, for you as a person, or for your future has taken something precious from you. From your view of such a terrifying event, they have taken your very soul, they have taken your life, and your heart feels empty; you have been broken and bruised, and part of you has been destroyed. When we suffer such horrific experiences, we begin to believe that our life is without hope, that we can never overcome what has happened to us, that we can never heal from the deep wounds in our soul. We may even begin to believe that our life is beyond salvaging.

Well, there is good news. Your life is worth salvaging, and there is Hope. You can take your life back. Through Biblical principles, love, and the healing power of Jesus Christ. Jesus Christ said, *"The thief cometh not, but for to steal, and to kill, and to destroy: I am come that they might have life, and that they might have it more abundantly"* (John 10:10). Your life can be salvaged and restored. For the principles and laws, we will be learning, salvage means "the act of saving; preservation from destruction, danger, or great calamity; deliverance from enemies."

Imagine an old historical home. At one time, a family lived in this home. and they were happy in the home, and they enjoyed the beauty and splendor of their home. For whatever reason, they moved out and moved on.. The building sat empty filling with dust; the once strong structure began to crumble. Rocks shattered the windows and graffiti covered its wood panels. Someone suggested that the old house be destroyed because of its condition. However, others realized the house still had potential, and they knew the home had a history. People had lived in it and enjoyed it before; so out of love for the old house, they decided to purchase the home and rescue it from destruction. We would describe such an act as salvaging the house. Just as the teddy bear represents something being taken from you, the house represents you as a person. You have potential. You have value. And you are worth salvaging. Therefore, Jesus Christ desires to salvage you; He desires to redeem you from the destroyer.

Once the house has been salvaged, the people who purchased it for salvage begin to restore it immediately. They work toward putting it back to its original state to making it livable once again.

The word restoration is another important word for us to know. Restoration means "the act of replacing in a former state, renewal, revival; re-establishment; as the restoration of friendship between enemies; the restoration of peace after war, recovery; renewal of health and soundness, recovery from a lapse or any bad state." Like the house, you can be restored and become the person God intended you to be. Your life can be made livable again. You are valuable beyond measure, and you have great potential. You are worthy of salvaging, and you are worthy of restoration.

Consider the teddy bear taken from the little girl, if we could capture it from the terrible person who took it from her, we would salvage it from the trash heap, mend it, restore it to its original condition, and return it to the little girl.

WHO TOOK THE TEDDY BEAR?

Satan is the ultimate enemy. He is the one behind all the destruction in your life. No, it was not him personally that stole from you, but it was his messenger or agent that allowed him or herself to be used as a tool of destruction. As Jesus said, *"The thief cometh not, but for to steal, and to kill, and to destroy."* Satan is the Thief. He stole from you; he attempted to take your life, to attack your innocence, to steal your self-value, and to rob you of your peace of mind and of your ability to trust. He has killed; that is, he has deprived you of life, the joy and hope of life. He has destroyed. The word destroyed means "to be cast down"; it is metaphoric of spiritual destruction. All of this is the work of Satan. He is the one behind the little girl's teddy bear being taken from her, and he is the one that desires to tear down the house.

IT IS NOT YOUR FAULT

Focus your thoughts on this truth, and write this on your heart: it is not your fault. We can trace the enemy's destructive activities all the way back to the beginning of time, back to the only perfect environment that ever existed on earth, the Garden of Eden. It was perfect in every way, and it was paradise on earth; yet, the enemy was able to enter in and break the trust of the first woman. Satan challenged the very Word of God, and he placed doubt in the woman's mind, "*. . . Yea hath God said ye shall not eat of the garden . . .*" through his deceitful efforts Satan was able to break the first woman's trust in God and His Word (Genesis 3:1). Satan still works in the same manner; if he has not yet broken your trust in God, he wants to. Of course, we know that Satan did convince the first woman to partake of the forbidden tree. Using our metaphor, we would say that Satan took the first woman's teddy bear from her, perhaps just as he has made an attack on your life and taken from you.

There are some important truths here for you to focus on. First of all, Satan had entered the woman's safe place. Secondly, he hid his true identity; he had disguised himself as a serpent. Thirdly, he lied to the woman, he promised something that he could not deliver; *"... ye shall be as gods..."* Fourthly, Satan's attack on the woman affected her other relationships; she *"... gave also unto her husband with her; and he did eat."* She also hid herself from God, the one that created her and loved her the most.

This evil is always at the center of Satan's agenda; to discourage us from trusting God, to steal all hope from us, to deprive us of a victorious life and, in the end, to destroy our dreams, our self-value, our future, and our relationships.

Perhaps some of these issues are at the heart of the things you have had to deal with in your own life. Satan's methods have not changed since his destructive attack on the first woman and family in the Garden of Eden. But just as God reached out to the first woman and her husband to salvage her and restore her, He is reaching out to you with hope, healing, love, and restoration.

CHRIST HAS POWER OVER SATAN

Through His vicarious death on the Cross, where He shed His blood and died for our sin and for the sin of the entire world, and through His victorious resurrection, Jesus Christ has defeated Satan, the enemy and all those who are Satan's workers and messengers. Jesus Christ says, *"I am come that they might have life, and that they might have it more abundantly."* The statement, *"I am come"* has the meaning of, "to reach; to arrive within reach of; to gain; to come so near as to be able to take or possess." It has the idea of being present right now. Jesus Christ makes himself available right now. He is within reach, and He is reaching out, offering abundant life.

Jesus Christ can help you take your life back. He has power over Satan, and He can help you confront all the issues and wounds of your life. He is the victor. He wants to earn your trust. He can rescue the teddy bear!

YOU AND YOUR TEDDY BEAR

We are using the teddy bear to represent our soul being taken by the enemy. May I share some truths with you about yourself? God created you as a Body, Soul, and Spirit. The body is self-explanatory: touch, taste, smell, sound, and sight. However, your body is your personal space. Your body contains your Soul and Spirit. The Bible refers to the body of a believer as a Temple, so your body is a sacred place. When our physical body is violated, it affects our Soul and Spirit. Biblically, you are a Soul, and you have a Body. Physical abuse, whether sexual or otherwise, is an attack on one's Body, Soul, and Spirit. The visible, physical wounds may heal, but it is the wounds of the Soul and Spirit that we struggle with the most.

The Tabernacle which consists of the Outer Court, the Inner Court, and the Most Holy Place reflectively illustrates our Body, Soul, and Spirit. As we have already mentioned, the Body is touch, sound, sight, and smell. The Soul is the seat of the mind, emotions (affections, heart), conscience, and reasoning (understanding right and wrong). Physical and emotional abuse affects the Soul, and physical abuse places wounds and scars on the Soul; it causes damage to the conscience, reasoning, emotions, and the mind. It causes the heart to break, it affects our emotions in that we put up barriers in relationships, and it affects our ability to reason and to trust.

The Spirit is the seat of Reverence, Prayer, Worship, Faith, and Hope. These are symbolized in the Tabernacle diagram as being in the Most Holy Place. Our Spirit is that part of us that communicates with God. Let's look at these words that describe the Spirit:

> **Reverence**: The way we view God.
>
> **Prayer**: Communication with God.
>
> **Worship**: How we respond to God. To worship God is to surrender to Him. That includes surrendering all of our hurts, heartaches, wounds, and sorrow.
>
> **Faith**: Trusting God.
>
> **Hope**: Believing with expectation that something good is going to happen.

Keep in mind that this description of the Temple is an example of how God created you: Body, Soul, and Spirit. The Most Holy Place is where God dwelt. In the most Holy Place was the Ark of the Covenant. Inside the Ark of the Covenant was the Manna, which fell from Heaven. This is an illustration of God's provision and is a Type of Jesus Christ in that He came to us from Heaven to provide our greatest need. Also inside the Ark of the Covenant is Aaron's rod that budded. This illustrates something that died, yet lived again. It is a representation of Jesus Christ in His death, burial, and resurrection. It also illustrates to us the life we can have in Jesus Christ; we can have a life of joy, peace, and victory after life has been taken from us by the enemy (John 10:10).

The Ten Commandments are also in the Ark. They represent that God has spoken. That He always keeps His word and that His Word is our source of hope and healing. His Word today is the person of Jesus Christ. On top of the Ark of the Covenant is the Mercy seat. This is where the blood of the sin sacrifice was placed. God told Moses, regarding the Mercy seat,

> *And there I will meet with thee, and I will commune with thee from above the mercy seat, from between the two cherubim's (angels) which are upon the ark of the testimony, of all things which I will give thee in commandment unto the children of Israel. (Exodus 25:22)*

Now, here is the most important point of what we are talking about. When we take all of our internal pains our anger, our bitterness, our pain, our resentment, the secrets of our most inner being, and the secrets we have never spoken out-loud, when we take them into the Spiritual realm of the most Holy place of our-selves, when we take the hurts of our Spirit into the presence of God with Reverence, Prayer, Worship, Faith, and Hope, that is when healing begins. In the end, everything in life is Spiritual, even the iniquities that have been committed against us. When we approach them spiritually from the Word of God, healing is possible for the Soul and Spirit.

Jesus Christ is the Healer of the Broken Hearted . . . the Giver of Liberty. Jesus Christ proclaimed at the beginning of His earthly ministry,

> *The Spirit of the Lord is upon me, because he hath anointed me to preach the gospel to the poor; he hath sent me to heal the brokenhearted, to preach deliverance to the captives, and recovering of sight to the blind, to set at liberty them that are bruised (crushed, hurt or broken). (Luke 4:18)*

RESTORE YOUR LIFE

Remember the teddy bear that was taken from the little girl? Now imagine having the power to rescue the teddy bear from the evil person that took it. Imagine someone as immense as God willing to help you rescue the teddy bear, mending it, and restoring it back to the little girl. In order to do this, there are some things you must do first. First, you must trust God, you must be willing to let Him help you, and you must be willing to open your heart completely to Him. Remember, He is the one that heals broken hearts, sets captives free, and binds up the broken. All that He asks of us is that we trust Him, and that we provide Him a chance to earn our trust. Are you ready to take back your life?

If you believe you are ready to do that, close your eyes and imagine yourself reaching out and taking back the teddy bear. Reach out in faith, keeping in mind that the teddy bear represents your life, a life of value, a life that is salvageable and restorable. Do you have it? Have you salvaged the Teddy Bear? If so, let's begin the restoration.

PERSONAL REFLECTIONS

What does the teddy bear represent to you?

_____

_____

_____

_____

What has been taken from you that you want to take back?

_____

_____

_____

_____

CHAPTER FOUR

PAST-PRESENT-FUTURE: WHAT I CAN CHANGE

WRITE THIS TRUTH ON YOUR heart: "I cannot change my past, I can't always change my circumstances, but I can change me." As we seek restoration for our lives, we must come to terms with what we can change and what we cannot change, we must determine what we have no control of, and what we do have control of. A close look at our circumstances will reveal that we can control more than we realize, and we can purposely make changes in our lives. We can be restored, and we can do so by following Biblical principles of transformation. Before we get to these principles, let's look at a portion of Scripture from which we draw these principles. Romans 11:33-36 says:

O the depth of the riches both of the wisdom and knowledge of God! how unsearchable are his judgments, and his ways past finding out! For who hath known the mind of the Lord? or who hath been his counsellor? Or who hath first given to him, and it shall be recompensed unto him again? For of him, and through him, and to him, are all things: to whom be glory forever. Amen.

This passage stresses both the ability and trustworthiness of God, and reveals the following:

1. He is rich in wisdom and knowledge. He is our creator. He not only knows what is necessary to restore you and me, but as our creator, He knows what we need.
2. His Judgments are unsearchable, and His ways are past finding out. Judgments: Ability to weigh and compare all the

facts connected with the subject and determine what is best. Ways: Manner of doing anything, or passage of getting from one place to another.

3. Romans 11:34 says, *"For who hath known the mind of the Lord? Or who hath been his counsellor."* There is no one like Jesus Christ, so there is no one better to consult for hope, healing, and restoration.

The following are Biblical laws (doctrines or precepts) on our topic of *Past – Present – Future: What I Can Change*:

THE LAW OF TRANSFORMATION

Romans 12:1-2 says,

I beseech you therefore, brethren, by the mercies of God, that ye present your bodies a living sacrifice, holy, acceptable unto God, which is your reasonable service. And be not conformed to this world: but be ye transformed by the renewing of your mind, that ye may prove what is that good, and acceptable, and perfect, will of God.

Notice the statement: " . . . *be ye transformed."* The word "transformed" means changed or renewed. The statement continues: " . . . *by the renewing of your mind."* Renewing means to make new again; repairing, re-establishing, reviving, renovating, restoring. You will recall that we began this lesson with the following quote: "I cannot change my past, I cannot always change my circumstances, but I can change me." Now, in your mind, add to that quote the following statement: "I can be transformed, I can be repaired, I can be made new, I can be restored, and I can live and love again."

The law of transformation is putting forth an effort in our thoughts and our actions to make changes to improve our lives. The way Scripture explains conforming and transforming is thought-provoking. Romans 12:2 says, *"And be not conformed to this world, but be ye transformed by the renewing of your mind."* Conformed means to be reduced to the likeness of, so to be conformed to the environment we are in, we don't have to put forth any effort at all. We can choose to do absolutely nothing and remain as we are. If we view ourselves as broken and damaged or wounded and discarded, we can choose to do nothing at all to improve or change ourselves and remain conformed to the way we think about ourselves. The point then is this: we will conform to the environment we are in by doing absolutely nothing. However, to be transformed requires an intentional strategy and effort. Being transformed, or changing what we can, requires a proven plan of action applied with faith, a renewing of our mind, and a change in our thinking and beliefs.

WHAT I CAN CHANGE

Let's begin this process by taking inventory of what I can change in my thinking, my beliefs, and ultimately in my life.

I CAN CHANGE MY RELATIONSHIP WITH GOD.

Our illustration of the Body, Soul, and Spirit illustrates that our Spirit is the platform of Faith, Hope, Reverence, Prayer, and Worship. Faith is my trust in God; Hope is my believing something good will result in my taking the right actions in my life. Prayer is my communicating with God. Worship is how I respond to God, which is primarily my surrendering of the hurts and burdens of my life to Him. Finally, reverence is my view of God.

Let's begin with reverence, your view of God. The truth is we cannot change ourselves for the better until we have a right relationship with Jesus Christ. We can, however, change our relationship with God, and we can have a strong relationship with him. Consider these important questions: do you view God as the loving heavenly father that He is, or do you have issues with God? Do you blame Him for any negative event in your life? Do you see God as your Creator and the one who loves you and wants to help you? Do you have a relationship with God at all? Is there anything in your relationship with God that needs to change?

If there is something you need to change, before you go any further, meditate on it now. Perhaps it would be good to write down your thoughts at this moment and talk those thoughts over with God.

My Thoughts about God:

_____

_____

_____

_____

What I need to change about my relationship with God:

_____

_____

_____

_____

I CAN CHANGE THE WAY I VIEW MY PAST.

In order to do this, I must come to terms with the fact that I cannot change my past. However, I can change the way I view my past, and I can change myself for the present and future. I must determine that I can learn from my past and then move on. My past can and will control my present life only if I allow it.

I CAN CHANGE THE WAY I VIEW MY PRESENT.

I can change my perception about my present circumstances and the way I view my life right now. In order to make these positive changes, I need to take inventory of what is available to me right now that will help me.

1. I have the Bible, God's Word, as a resource to help me make changes in the way I view my present.
2. I have prayer, access to communicating with God about everything in my life.

(List four more resources and opportunities available to you.)

3. _____
4. _____
5. _____
6. _____

I CAN CHANGE THE WAY I VIEW MYSELF.

God created me in His image and in His likeness. Psalm 139:14 says, *"I am fearfully and wonderfully made."* The word fearfully means in a manner to impress, admiration and astonishment. The word wonderfully means in a manner to excite wonder or surprise. View yourself with the understanding that God loves you that He has a purpose for your life, and He loves you unconditionally.

I CAN CHANGE THE EMOTIONS THROUGH WHICH
I VIEW THOSE WHO HAVE HURT ME.

Making this change in your life will require a concentrated effort, trust in God, and a willingness to release some emotions that could be causing you to remain trapped by defeat. But making this modification will truly be life altering.

However, you can change the way you view your past and the way you view those in the past that have hurt you. A hard truth is that we sometimes allow people in our past to shackle us and keep us in bondage to the past. Some of these people are gone, and some of them barely think about us; yet, we allow them to control us. So, write this on your heart: "I can change the emotions through which I view those who have hurt me."

1. View people with love, not hate.

The Lord Jesus Christ taught us this principle in the Sermon on the Mount. In Matthew 5:44, He instructed us to " . . . *love your enemies, bless them that curse you, do good to them that hate you, and pray for them which despitefully use you and persecute you.*" We know that Jesus not only told us this, but He also lived this law in His own life, as He would never ask us to do something that He was unwilling to do Himself. Choosing to follow this one Biblical law will change you and your life.

2. I can change the emotion of bitterness for the emotion of forgiveness.

Someone said, "Bitterness is the only poison that destroys its own container." How true that is! We must "put off" our bitterness and choose to forgive those who have hurt us. Forgiving those who have hurt us sets us free from the bondage of bitterness.

3. I can change the emotion of malice (a desire to do harm) for the emotion of goodwill.

Instead of desiring to see harm or to cause harm to come to those who have hurt me, I desire goodwill to come their way. Jesus said it this way: *"bless them that curse you, do good to them that hate you, and pray for them which despitefully use you and persecute you."*

4. I can exchange clamor (outcry about the past and evil speaking) for only speaking about my blessings, about my goals, and about the people God has placed in my life now that love me and want to see me be victorious.

In my years of ministry, I have learned that one way to tell whether or not someone has truly forgiven someone or not is by what they talk about in their normal conversations. If they continually speak evil of people that have been in their lives, then they have not truly forgiven those people. And if they continually speak evil of people from their past, then they are allowing those people to keep them in the bondage of bitterness.

Joseph in the Old Testament offers us an example of true forgiveness. Joseph was hated by his own brothers. He was sold by them into slavery, and from there his life spiraled downward for years. You may recall the events of Joseph's life. After twenty years, he was reunited with his father and his brothers. Eventually, Joseph's father died, and his brothers feared he would kill them, but Genesis 50:19-21 supplies us with Joseph's response to their fears.

> *Fear not: for am I in the place of God? But as for you, ye thought evil against me; but God meant it unto good, to bring to pass, as it is this day, to save*

much people alive. Now therefore fear ye not: I will nourish you, and your little ones. And he comforted them, and spake kindly unto them.

Notice that Joseph practiced the law of exchanging clamor, or outcry about the past and evil speaking, to blessings. He comforted the very family members who had done evil to him, and he spoke kindly to them. Again, I emphasize I cannot change my past; I cannot change the wrongs done against me. I can change my clamor and my speaking evil about those who have done evil against me. I can speak kindly about them or not at all. I can focus my conversations more on the blessings I have today, the goals I have for tomorrow, and the people in my life right at this moment that love me and want the best for me.

5. I can change my wrath (anger that seeks vengeance) to desiring to use my life to help and serve others.

Instead of trying to get even or trying to seek vengeance on someone from my past, I can search out people and opportunities to help make someone else's life better in my present. Instead of focusing on my past, I can focus on my present and making my life better, which will also be a blessing to those in my life now.

I CAN CHANGE THE WAY I VIEW MY FUTURE.

I can choose to view my future with hope and promise. My past is past, but my future is before me. I have some control over the decisions I make about my future and about the life I'm going to live today. I can set goals for tomorrow. I can take inventory of opportunities for my future:

What does God have for me to do?

_____

_____

_____

_____

What relationships do I have right now on which I can build?

_____

_____

_____

Who can I help?

_____

_____

_____

What can I learn?

_____

_____

_____

_____

I CAN CHANGE WHOM I PERMIT TO INFLUENCE OR CONTROL ME BY DETHRONING THE EVIL KINGS AND QUEENS IN MY LIFE.

This notion is one of the greatest powers you have in your life as an adult. You can choose whom you believe. You can choose whom you permit to influence or control you. As a friend of mine would say, "You can choose who you let in your head!" Don't listen to people that try to keep you down, those who keep dragging you back to your past and think that their calling in life is to discourage you and remind you of all your former pains. This is the law of changing who influences and controls you. Consider the people that influence or control you, and think about who you permit to rule and reign in your thoughts and emotions.

This is a life changing truth. I ask you to trust the Biblical foundation of this truth, consider it carefully, and meditate on it with all of your heart. In 2 Chronicles 14:1-6, we find that after a long line of evil kings and queens, Asa took the throne. King Asa was a descendant of King David. Scripture tells us that Asa began to reign: *"So Abijah (Asa's father) slept with his fathers (died)... and Asa his son reigned in his stead"* (2 Chronicles 14:1). Asa began to reign; he immediately began to take charge of the situation. King Asa was determined to make things better for the people, so when King Asa took the throne he made some significant changes. I will list some of those changes, and they will lead us to our law of changing who influences us.

1. King Asa removed the altars of the strange gods (most of which his fore-fathers had brought in).
2. King Asa dethroned the evil queen in his life.

2 Chronicles 15:16 records this: *"And also concerning Maachah the mother of Asa the king, he removed her from being queen, because she had made an idol in a grove: and Asa cut down her idol, and stamped it, and burnt it at the brook Kidron."* The important point of the text for us is found in the statement, *"... he removed her from being queen..."* This is the law of changing who you permit to influence you. Maachah was still Asa's grandmother. He could not remove her biologically from his life, but he could remove her from the throne of influence and control. Considering the circumstances, I don't question that he loved her. But, Asa had to choose whom he would permit to influence him and whom he would permit to influence the people entrusted to his care as king. Asa chose not to allow Maachah to rule in his life or in the lives of his people.

You cannot permit the person who hurt you, the person who took that which is precious from you, to reign and rule in your life. You. Must. Dethrone. Them. You alone have the power to do so. You can begin to reign in your own life; you can begin to take control of how you respond to the circumstances in your life! You can remove the evil kings and queens from their places of influence and control in your life. That does not mean you will no longer love them or care about them or want them to do well. You should want these things. That is not to say that you should remove them from your life completely. That might not be possible. However, you must determine not to grant them access to your thoughts and emotions. You may not be able to remove them from your past, and you may not be able to completely remove them from your mind, but you can remove them from ruling in your thoughts and emotions. If they are still hurting you with memories or words and deeds, then you must not permit them to rule your thoughts and emotions.

Find the strength that Asa had in dethroning the queen. Maachah was the queen that had introduced the false god Asherah (ash-ay-raw). This idol was the goddess of sexual perversion and was extremely evil. The root meaning of her name is horror. So, we make the application that Maachah brought sexual perversion into the environment of the people. Scripture tells us that when Asa began to reign he " . . . *cut down the groves*" (2 Chronicles 14:3). This passage references Asa removing the goddess Asherah from Israel. The whole purpose of this book is to help you with the process of dethroning those who have hurt you and removing them from ruling in your thoughts and emotions, to help you end the horrors that the evil kings and queens have caused you, and to bequeath you with the principles and the confidence to cut down the groves of evil.

You can change who you permit to influence or control you!

God has told us to pray and that gives us liberty to ask Him how to pray. God will tell us what is causing our hurt and what to do with that hurt. Ask God to send you thoughts, and then write them down. Be prepared to deal with and act in obedience where those thoughts are concerned.

Ask God to guide you to the Scripture, which you may meditate on and use those words to help you heal.

Am I currently permitting someone to hurtfully reign over my thoughts and emotions?

_____

_____

_____

Past-Present-Future: What I Can Change

Who is this person(s)?

_____

_____

_____

_____

Is this person(s) in my past or in my present?

_____

_____

_____

_____

How are they affecting (infecting) me?

_____

_____

_____

_____

What action can I take to dethrone them from my thoughts and emotions?

_____

_____

What are some verses and Biblical principles that will help me accomplish this?

Along with Jesus Christ, who can help me accomplish this and hold me accountable?

I will pray about this in the following way:

Actions I will take today:

_____

_____

_____

_____

HOW I CAN CHANGE ME

We have examined seven laws of personal change, now we must implement personal change. Realize that Jesus Christ is the one that does the transforming.

2 Corinthians 5:17 says, *"Therefore if any man be in Christ, he is a new creature (creation): old things are passed away; behold, all things are become new."* Jesus Christ empowers us to make the changes necessary to build better lives. Ultimately, He does the changing, and it all begins with permitting Him to change our hearts.

The second step is to surrender our self to Him, with all of our hurts, heartaches, pain, disappointments, fears, and weaknesses. We must surrender, that is what true Biblical worship is all about. It is surrendering ourselves, just as we are, to God just as He is.

Thirdly, know what you can change, what God has to change, and what cannot be changed. As we discussed in this lesson, we cannot change our past, but we can change our perception of the past.

Fourthly, decide to do what is necessary for the changes to take place in your life. The Apostle Paul, who needed many positive changes in his life, said, *"I can do all things through Christ which strengtheneth me"* (Philippians 4:13). The two most powerful words in this verse are not, *"I Can"* The most powerful words in Paul's statement are, *" . . . through Christ which strengtheneth me."* Jesus Christ can and will provide you the strength to make the changes in your life that will ultimately transform your life. Are you ready to make the changes that you can make?

PERSONAL REFLECTIONS

Things I know I cannot change:

_____

_____

_____

_____

Things in my life I believe God can change:

_____

_____

_____

_____

Action I need to take:

_____

_____

_____

_____

CHAPTER FIVE

THE POWER OF FORGIVENESS

ARCHIBALD HART SAID: "FORGIVENESS IS surrendering my right to hurt you for hurting me." Another wise person said: "To determine not to forgive someone is like drinking poison and hoping the other person is going to die." Of course, we realize that to forgive someone who has committed terrible acts of evil against us is easier said than done. Yet coming to the place of being able to forgive those who have committed evil against you is one of the greatest victories in your life journey of grace.

Like many of us, the Apostle Paul was a man that had to confront guilt in his own life, and he did so victoriously. Not only did Paul have to deal with the guilt of his own sins of the past, but he also had to confront the effects of people who had committed evil against him. There is a man by the name of Alexander that caused Paul great harm; in 2 Timothy 14, Paul conveys to Timothy the level of harm Alexander caused and the deep emotional pain it caused him. Paul describes the situation *"Alexander the coppersmith did me much evil . . ."* We don't know all the details of what Alexander the coppersmith did against Paul, but it was a sin committed against him, possibly slander, other Scripture indicates that Alexander taught blasphemous teachings that hurt Paul's ministry.

GUILT ASSOCIATED WITH EVIL

Heartache is in the aftermath of the evil acts. The people who have had evil committed against them and their loved ones have to deal with the sorrow, and usually, depending on the evil that has been committed against them, they also have to deal with guilt and shame. There are several reasons for this.

Often in cases of molestation the molester has told the victim that they are the one at fault, and they are the one to blame. The victim is often threatened that horrible things will happen if they tell anyone.

I have counseled women who have been raped that were told the rape would not have occurred if they had been dressed differently or had not walked the way they did or been in the place they were in. Such responses only make matters worse for the victim that has already been traumatized. These types of statements are false. Evil people commit evil deeds. I have also counseled adults that were molested as children, some of them by fathers and step fathers; some of these evil men told their own children that the molestation happened because of something that they had done wrong. However, what I perceive as even more malicious is that some perpetrators told their children or step children they molested them because they love them. Only a person with a malicious soul would make such a statement.

The reality is that scores of people struggle with the challenge of carrying guilt for sins that were not committed by them but for the horrible deeds that were committed against them. If you feel that you are carrying guilt from evil that has been committed against you, look closely at these biblical truths.

SATAN IS A LIAR AND AN ACCUSER

John 8:44 says:

> ... He (Satan) is a murderer from the beginning, and abode not in truth, because there is no truth in him. When he speaketh a lie, he speaketh of his own: for he is a liar and the father of it." Corresponding to that, Revelation 12:10 says, "And I heard a loud voice saying in Heaven, Now is come salvation, and strength, and the kingdom of our God, and the power of his Christ: for the accuser of our brethren is cast down, which accused them before God day and night.

Take a note here of Satan's future, some day he will be chained and cast into the very pit of Hell. Think of that for a moment; his future is terrifying, but your future can be victorious in Jesus Christ.

Satan is the enemy, and he wants to defeat you in every possible way. He will resort to using your past, he will use sins committed against you to discourage you, to rob you of your dreams, your hope, your peace, and your value as a child of God. Make no mistake about this, God WILL NOT use sins committed against you to discourage you. But Satan, the great liar, accuser, and life destroyer will heap guilt on you; he will even use the person that committed an evil act against you to persuade you that it is your fault, that you are really the guilty party. Don't you believe this lie! Don't believe Satan's deception! When Satan accuses you that means you are innocent because he will eternally be a liar.

EVIL COMMITTED AGAINST YOU IS NOT YOUR FAULT

IT'S NOT YOUR FAULT! The sin and the guilt of the sin were placed solely on the evil person who committed the crime against you, not on you. God is just, and He will not hold you accountable for sins others have committed.

When Jonah was running from God, he boarded a boat for Tarshish, God allowed the boat to enter a terrible storm because of Jonah's sin. The other men on the boat were innocent, but they had to endure the storm on their journey. Notice what Jonah 1:14 says, *"Wherefore they cried unto the Lord, and said, We beseech thee, O Lord, we beseech thee, let us not perish for this man's life, and lay not upon us innocent blood; for thou O Lord, hast done as it pleased thee."* We know that in the end Jonah went overboard and spent three days and three nights on an ocean voyage in the depths of a whale's belly.

Like the innocent men on Jonah's boat, you have had to endure the heartache, sorrow, and pain of someone else's sin. You have had to endure wounds of the soul, spirit and possibly of the body because someone committed an act of evil against you. But that does not make you guilty of anything, just as those men being on the same boat with Jonah did not make them guilty of Jonah's sin.

My friend, I know from counseling scores of people, this is an important point I want you to grasp. The evil committed against you was not laid to your account. If you feel any guilt from someone committing evil against you, you are not the guilty party, they are! The blame is not on you, but on the *one who committed evil* against you. You are not to be blamed.

GOD LOVES YOU

God loves you no matter what; He cares that sin has been committed against you, and He cares that you have been hurt, that your heart has been broken, and that your spirit has been wounded. God wants you to trust Him with all of your suffering, including the ones caused by people who committed sins against you. And God does not want you to carry the guilt of those sins.

YOU ARE VALUABLE TO GOD

In my counseling ministry, I have learned that one of the things that people who struggle with any kind of guilt struggle with is self-value. Well, no matter what has been done to you or against you, you have great value and great potential in God's eyes. God's Word teaches us that you are *"fearfully and wonderfully made."* God's Word teaches us that you are a treasure in an earthen vessel (physical body). We will have a chapter on this later, but for now I just want to remind you of your self-value.

Paul's letter to Timothy and other examples in Scripture provide ways to forgive those who have committed evil against you. We will see that we can forgive those who committed evil against us, that we possess the power to forgive them and that we can live our own life in victory.

We read in 1 Timothy 1:18-20:

This charge I commit unto thee, son Timothy, according to the prophecies which went before on thee, that thou by them mightest war a good warfare; Holding faith, and a good conscience; which some having put away concerning faith have made shipwreck: Of whom is Hymenaeus and Alexander; whom I have delivered unto Satan, that they may learn not to blaspheme.

Notice Paul's words to young Timothy in verse 20, " . . . *and Alexander; whom I have delivered unto Satan, that they may learn not to blaspheme."* The purpose of Paul's letter is twofold. First, to instruct Timothy on how to confront various situations in life and in the ministry; as Paul learned we must at times confront people who commit evil against us. So, Paul approaches this matter by warning Timothy to be on guard and by teaching him what he had learned from his own experience. Secondly, Paul teaches him how to forgive.

DELIVER THEM UNTO SATAN

Paul imparts the first step in dealing with someone who has committed evil against us in the following statement, "*. . . and Alexander; whom I have delivered unto Satan, that they may learn not to blaspheme.*" The key word is "delivered"; it means released, transferred or passed from one to another. The principle here is that Paul released Hymenaeus and Alexander to Satan. He was not going to allow them or the evil, which they had committed against him, to fill his thoughts or have control over his life. Hymenaeus and Alexander's influence and actions came from Satan, so Paul delivered them back to the realm of Satan, and this was the realm of life that Paul chose not to visit in or dwell in.

From Paul's teaching we discover the first step to forgiving those who have committed evil against us is to deliver them, to release them, and to relinquish them back to Satan, the one that has ultimately committed evil against you through his power of influence in the life of those who wounded you.

THE LORD'S REWARD

We find Paul's second step in 2 Timothy 4:14 at the close of this letter to Timothy. The fact that Paul mentions Alexander a second time to Timothy conveys to us that Paul was deeply wounded in his spirit by the evil act that Alexander had committed against him. The passage also reminds us that Paul sought to warn Timothy and teach him to confront such situations. Notice that Paul never mentions what Alexander had done to him to anyone else other than Timothy and that was primarily for the purposes of teaching and to warn Timothy to beware of Alexander. There is a lesson in Paul's example here: when we have truly forgiven someone, we stop talking about them and what they have done to us. We turn the evil person and their evil deed over to the God, so we no longer have to constantly discuss what they have done, or even bring them up in conversation.

In 2 Timothy 4:14, Paul writes, "*Alexander the coppersmith did me much evil: the Lord reward him according to his works.*" Not only did Paul deliver Alexander to Satan but he also released all vengeance to God. The word *"reward"* means to give in return, either good or evil. This was not done so Alexander could receive a prize. This was done so that God could deal with Alexander in His own timing and in His own way. Paul did not say, I will get even, or I will seek vengeance for the evil Alexander has committed against me. No, Paul said I will let God deal with him. God will take care of settling the score. Paul turned the "getting even" with Alexander over to God and Paul focused on his own spiritual growth and on living and loving again, and he focused on the friends and family that were in his life that he knew loved him and cared for him in his present. You can do the same, you have a life to live and there are people that love you. Forgive, let go, live, and love again.

CONFRONTING EMOTIONS

We discussed this in our lesson on "Past – Present – Future What I Can Change." We will further our discussion in greater depth here in Ephesians 4:30-34 which says,

And grieve not the Holy Spirit of God, whereby ye are sealed unto the day of redemption. Let all bitterness (anger in its most poisonous state), and wrath (anger that seeks vengeance), and anger, and clamour (loud and continued noise), and evil speaking, be put away from you, with all malice (a disposition to injure others).

The Apostle Paul writes under the inspiration of the Holy Spirit and from his own personal experience to put away the emotions and the behavior that is generated by the evil committed against you. Bitterness, wrath, malice, and anger are emotions; clamor and evil speaking are behaviors that are generated by the emotions. All of these things grieve the Holy Spirit, and they also keep us in bondage to the evil that has been committed against us, which keeps us from living the victorious life that is available to us.

We must Biblically confront these emotions and actions, and as Paul encourages us we must put them "away." The word "away" means at a distance, to separate, to cast from or away. This is exactly what Paul had to do in his own life.

Paul delivered Alexander to Satan, thus separating himself from Alexander and the bitterness, anger, wrath, and malice he might have kindled in his own heart. Then Paul released Alexander to the judgment of the Lord, separating himself from Alexander and removing himself so the Lord could reward

Alexander " ... *according to his works.*" Don't try to do God's job. You can't do it as well as He can, and your efforts will only frustrate you and keep you defeated. Let God take care of the vengeance.

Once we have *"put away"* the emotions we have toward the person that has committed evil against us, once we have separated ourselves from the bitterness, anger, vengeance, and malice ... we can then move on to the next step in restoring our lives from the evil that has been committed against us.

FORGIVING

My friend Suzi F., who is a victim of abuse but is now a victor, said, "Forgiveness is the key that opens the door that hate closed." Forgiveness is also the key that opens the door that anger closed. Let me state clearly that this is easier said than done, and I'm certain that Paul struggled with forgiving Alexander. But from what we read in Scripture, Paul was able to forgive Alexander and move on with his life and ministry.

After he encourages us to *"put away"* all bitterness, anger, clamour, evil speaking, and malice in verse 31, Paul continues in Ephesians 4:32 with these words, *"And be ye kind one to another, tenderhearted, forgiving one another, even as God for Christ's sake hath forgiven you."* The first part of Paul's statement reveals to us that true forgiveness, the kind of forgiveness toward others that unlocks chains of bitterness, anger, and malic begins in the heart. The words *"and be ye kind"* implies that we need to change our own heart, our feelings, or emotions toward the person or people that have committed evil against us. We must change our hearts from bitterness, anger, and malice to *"kind ... (and) tenderhearted."*

So, you may be asking how Paul was able to change his own heart. How was he able to *"put away"* the emotions of bitterness, anger, and malice that he had toward Alexander so that he could forgive and begin living and loving again? Paul reveals the answer in his own testimony. In 1 Timothy, before Paul mentions that he delivered Hymenaeus and Alexander unto Satan, Paul writes of how thankful he is that Jesus Christ changed his own heart and life and provided him with the ability to live and love again. We read in 1 Timothy 1:12-17:

> *And I thank Christ Jesus our Lord, who hath enabled me, for that he counted me faithful, putting me into the ministry; Who was before a blasphemer, and a persecutor, and injurious: but I obtained mercy, because I did it ignorantly in unbelief. And the grace of our Lord was exceeding abundant with faith and love which is in Christ Jesus. This is a faithful saying, and worthy of all acceptation, that Christ Jesus came into the world to save sinners; of whom I am chief. Howbeit for this cause I obtained mercy, that in me first Jesus Christ might shew forth all longsuffering, for a pattern to them which should hereafter believe on him to life everlasting. Now unto the King eternal, immortal, invisible, the only wise God, be honour and glory for ever and ever. Amen.*

I love this passage of Scripture. There are several key points to make here. First, notice that Paul mentions his own spiritual condition before his conversion; he needed God's forgiveness. And once Paul received God's forgiveness for his own sin he was incredibly thankful.

Notice also the words "*. . . that in me first Jesus Christ might shew forth all longsuffering, for a pattern to them that should hereafter believe on him to life everlasting.*" Paul realized that in God's forgiving him of his own sin, God set forth a pattern of how he could forgive others. That pattern included being longsuffering toward people that have committed evil against him. Longsuffering means to be patient, to endure. When it comes to forgiving someone that has committed evil against us, even in the worst imaginable ways, we must endure them and what they have done. We must endure the memories of their actions and we must endure them personally, but, through our own determined endurance, we come to the place of forgiving them.

Paul was able to forgive Alexander for the evil committed against him because he had learned from the longsuffering God had expressed to him. And Paul could forgive Alexander because of the pattern of forgiveness God had demonstrated toward Paul in forgiving him of all the evil he had committed. Through this forgiveness of Alexander, the Apostle Paul was able to release himself of all the bondage associated with un-forgiveness, and he was able to move forward and grow spiritually, living and loving his life in victory without the distractions and bondage of un-forgiveness toward someone that had committed evil against him.

Unshackle yourself from the bondage that keeps you attached to the person or people who have committed evil against you. Forgive them and live and love again in victory!

FORGIVENESS THROUGH PRAYER

As Paul would have done, you need to take your situation to the LORD, and in your own heart you need to deliver the person or persons that have hurt you over to the LORD and let God deal with any vengeance or payment they have coming to them for their evil deeds. Then you need to prayerfully forgive them for what they have done to you. In forgiving them, consider the joy of knowing that you are forgiven in Jesus Christ and God is willing to forgive you and I because He loves His only begotten Son Jesus Christ, then we should be able to forgive those who have hurt us. True forgiveness must come from our heart, but you will find that forgiving those who have hurt you will make you free.

THE POWER TO FORGIVE

Because you are the one that was hurt, you have within you a power, a power bestowed upon you by God to freely choose your emotions and your actions. You can choose right this moment to let go, to forgive from within your own heart the person or people who have hurt you. You can choose to forgive and move forward with a life free of anger, wrath, malice, and bitterness to live in victory, or you can choose to remain as you are. Forgiveness doesn't make your circumstances better, and it won't make the person who has hurt you better, but forgiveness will make you better.

PERSONAL REFLECTIONS

What helps me realize it's not my fault?

_____

_____

_____

_____

I know God loves me because:

_____

_____

_____

_____

I choose to forgive:

_____

_____

_____

_____

I will deliver them back to Satan by:

_____

_____

_____

_____

I will not seek vengeance, I will release them to God and let God execute His judgment as He deems right; I will move forward in victory to live and love again!

Signed _____ Date_____

Today I will put away any emotions of anger, bitterness, hate, and malice I have toward the person(s) who have hurt me.

Signed _____ Date_____

To forgive this person I will work toward changing these emotions in my heart:

_____

_____

_____

_____

I'm thankful that God has done these things in my life:

_____

_____

_____

_____

CHAPTER SIX

QUESTIONS FROM THE HEART, ANSWERS FROM GOD

NO MATTER WHAT OUR DIFFICULT experiences have been we usually find ourselves with unanswered questions and sometimes we have questions we don't know how to ask or who to ask. Some of these questions burden our hearts and weigh on our minds as we strive to sort through them. Some of us have been told that it is wrong to ask questions and that it is especially wrong to question God. So, we fear the idea of asking God "Why?"! However, the Bible confirms that even Jesus Christ asked God the Father "Why?" While enduring the Cross, Jesus cried out, *"My God, My God, why hast thou forsaken me?"* (Matthew 27:46).

Another valuable example of someone in the Bible that asked questions is Job. Outside of Jesus Christ who suffered the trauma of the Crucifixion, dying for the sin of the world on the Cross, Job suffered more physically, emotionally, and spiritually than any other person recorded in Scripture. Job, however, did not directly ask God any questions. He did ask his friends some extraordinarily powerful and thought-provoking questions, such as, *"Why died I not from the womb? Why did I not give up the ghost when I came out of the belly?"* (Job 3:11). We see by the wording of these questions that Job did not ask to die, but he did ask why he was ever born. Job also asked his friends, *"What is my strength, that I should hope? And what is mine end, that I should prolong my life?"* (Job 6:11). Job also asked, *"Where is now my hope?"* (Job 16:15). These are questions from the depths of a broken heart and a grieving spirit.

Just as Job had questions from his heart, I have found that everyone who has experienced trauma has questions as well. And I have learned that when we are in a situation that the questions are difficult to ask, it also means that the answers will be difficult as well. Although our personal circumstances differ, and everyone struggles differently from the effects of abuse, we know that the Word of God gives us hope and understanding. Hebrews 4:12 explains, *"For the word of God is quick, and powerful, and sharper than any two-edged sword, piercing even to the dividing asunder of soul and spirit, and of the joints and marrow, and is a discerner of the thoughts and intents of the heart."* This important truth tells us that the Word of God (Bible) is alive, it is a living book. It is powerful and able to pierce into the secret places of our hearts, and it is able to help us separate what is physical (Body), what is emotional (Soul), and what is spiritual (Spirit). And the Bible has the power to supply us with discernment or understanding of our thoughts and emotions.

As mentioned earlier, Job did not directly ask God questions, though God did answer Job's questions in Job 38-41. By enlisting the help of friends who have suffered physical, emotional, verbal, and sexual abuse, we have compiled a list of questions that we will attempt to answer from the Bible. Some questions are not covered here because they are dealt with in great detail as chapters in this book, such as: How do I move on with my life? How do I forgive? How do I know I have forgiven completely?

The questions are not in any particular order, but we hope you will find the answers helpful and healing, so you can move forward with living and loving again.

QUESTION: WHY ME?

Certainly, this was at the heart of all of Job's questions, and this is probably the most prevalent question of all. Although some victims of abuse may never utter the words out loud to another human being, this is still the question that weighs heavy in the heart of every abuse victim. And the answer is as difficult as the question.

SATAN IS BEHIND EVERY EVIL ACT

I assure you the answer to the "Why me?" question is not because of anything you have or have not done. You have not done anything to deserve abuse! But because of whom Satan is and what he has done since the beginning of creation, searching out ways to hurt people in every way possible. You happened to be one of many who were on Satan's radar.

SATAN'S INFLUENCES

His demons influenced the abuser who carried out the evil acts that hurt you. As mentioned earlier, Satan is behind every evil act, he is the driving force in the life of everyone that commits acts of evil. This point is confirmed in Job 1:14-15:

And there came a messenger unto Job, and said, The oxen were plowing, and the asses feeding beside them: And the Sabeans fell upon them, and took them away; yea, they have slain the servants with the edge of the sword; and I only am escaped alone to tell thee.

The Sabeans were sun worshippers; they were evil people. Bible historians agree that they were alcoholics and dealt in the slave trade. The Sabeans also worshipped Ashteroth, who was a goddess of sexual perversion. Satan used the Sabeans to bring destruction upon Job's family. We also see in Job 1:17 that Satan used a group of Chaldeans for destruction.

While he was yet speaking, there came also another, and said, The Chaldeans made out three bands, and fell upon the camels, and have carried them away, yea, and slain the servants with the edge of the sword; and I only am escaped alone to tell thee.

The Chaldeans were an aggressive people who took pleasure in starting wars.

It is not your fault. You did nothing to deserve this. Ultimately it is Satan's fault and the person that allowed his or herself to be influenced by him. You are not to be blamed, Satan is and the person that allowed his or herself to be used as his tool for destruction.

You have done nothing wrong. Satan has. Through the work of his demons and the actions of someone influenced by them, Satan has attacked you in the most destructive way. Just as he did in Job's day, Satan continues, *"going to and fro in the earth, and from walking up and down in it"* (Job 1:7). 1 Peter 5:8 explains *". . . your adversary the devil, as a roaring lion, walketh about, seeking whom he may devour."*

Job was *". . . perfect and upright, and one that feared God . . ."* and so Satan made Job a target for his destructive practices. Perhaps the answer to "Why me?" is in the Biblical truth that Satan is evil, and he attacks anyone he can in any way he possibly can. He has legions of Demons who work on his behalf for the cause of destruction in the lives of the people God loves, and you happen to be one of the people God loves. Perhaps the most reasonable answer to the question "Why me?" is because *". . . your adversary the devil, as a roaring lion, walketh about, seeking whom he may devour."*

QUESTION: IS THERE SOMETHING WRONG WITH ME? IS THERE SOMETHING ABOUT ME THAT MAKES PEOPLE DRAWN TO HURT ME?

This is probably a question that Job also had in his heart. Some of Job's trouble was brought on by the actions of people; he also endured the effects of nature, which was influenced by Satan. So, let me do my best to answer the question: Is there something wrong with me? Absolutely not! The struggle is that we all live in Satan's world, and he is always on the attack. When he uncovers an opening in the Hedge of protection, he enters in and attacks. I answer this question with another question in hopes to offer you some assurance that there is nothing wrong with you. Was there something wrong with Eve that Satan would possess a snake and enter the Garden of Eden to abuse her emotionally, causing her to distrust God? No there was not.

The fact is that God loved Eve, and He loves you. Satan attacked Eve when he saw an opportunity just as he attacked you when he saw that opportunity, and he used a willing snake in both instances. So, let me use this opportunity to assure you that God loves you and always keep in mind the fact that Satan hates everything that God loves.

QUESTION: WHERE WAS GOD WHEN I NEEDED HIM MOST?

This is also a question Job struggled with during the darkest time of his life. Notice what Job said to his friend Eliphaz, *"Oh that I knew where I might find him! that I might come even to his seat!"* (Job 23:3). *"Behold, I go forward, but he is not there; and backward, but I cannot perceive him: On the left hand, where he doth work, but I cannot behold him: he hideth himself on the right hand, that I cannot see him"* (Job 23:8-9).

Let me do my best to produce a Biblical answer to this question: Where was God when I needed him most? First, let's begin with an important truth. God is not the one who hurt you. God loves you and created you for himself and for the purpose of having a relationship with you that is based on trust and love. Satan hates anyone God loves, and, therefore, he seeks to destroy the trust and love we place in God.

One of the lies Satan places into the heart of every abuse victim is that God does not love you and is not there for you. This lie often distorts the abused person's view of God. Therefore, it is important to confirm in your heart that God is not the one who hurt you. The person who abused you is selfish, evil, and influenced by Satan and his demons. God is none of those things.

God was there, He protected you in that He spared your life, and He is here now and wants to help you. God desires to earn your trust, and He desires that you believe that He loves you. Jesus Christ was there, He was weeping for you, and His heart was breaking because He loves you and grieves when you grieve. Close your eyes and ask God to tell you that He was there. Many times, He will bring thoughts to your mind that He was with you, and He will provide you with comfort and strength now so that you can move forward with your life in victory.

Notice what Job continued to say to his friend Eliphaz,

> *But he knoweth the way that I take: when he hath tried me, I shall come forth as gold. My foot hath held his steps, his way have I kept, and not declined. Neither have I gone back from the commandment of his lips; I have esteemed the words of his mouth more than my necessary food. (Job 23:10-12)*

In this passage, Job confirms that even though he could not see God, he was still going to do what he knew to be right, and he was still going to love and trust God's Word. He believed that victory was possible. Perhaps one of the most powerful statements that Job made was when he spoke to God toward the end of his ordeal, *"I have heard of thee by the hearing of the ear: but now mine eye seeth thee"* (Job 42:5).

As we discussed in the chapter "Past-Present-Future, What I Can Change," we cannot change our past, but we can transform the way we interpret our past. Will you consider this thought? Perhaps you did not see God while you were being abused, but will you see Him now? Will you open your heart up to Him? Will you trust Him with your life now?

One of my favorite quotes from Job is found in Job 13:15, *"Though he slay me, yet will I trust in him: but I will maintain mine own ways before him. He also shall be my salvation..."* God was there in the past and just as important He is here now in your present, He loves you, and He wants you to trust Him for help and healing. Close your eyes, meditate in your heart, and see Jesus Christ standing before you with the wounds of Calvary on His body. He is reaching out to you, offering healing for your broken heart, deliverance from the captivity of your mind, and liberty from the bondage of defeat! Now reach out and receive His love.

QUESTION: WHY DO I STAY WITH OR RETURN TO MY ABUSER?

This question is approached with much prayer and thought. For over thirty years I have taught a lesson I refer to as the Four Human Needs. The four needs I share in the lesson are as follows:

1. I need someone to love me;
2. I need to feel important;

3. I need hope; and
4. I want to live, or I need a purpose for my life.

Two truths come to mind as we consider our question, "Why do I return to my abuser?" The first truth is that abusers know that we all have these four human needs, although they may not realize they know this. The second truth is that because we have these four human needs some of us are willing to suffer physical and emotional pain to have any or all of these human needs fulfilled. So, an abuser takes advantage of the four human needs in a warped way, usually not even realizing what he is doing. I will also suggest here that an abuser has his own issues about the four human needs being fulfilled in his own life, so it is a vicious emotional circle in the life of the abuser and in the life of the one being abused. I do not make this statement to defend any abuser, just pointing out a fact.

So, let's examine the four human needs:

HUMAN NEED: I NEED SOMEONE TO LOVE ME.

This is such a strong emotional need that a woman in an abusive relationship, who may not feel anyone else would ever love her because of some physical blemish, something from her past, or another weakness, which her abuser points out to her, often is willing to accept abuse for a false sense of love. Therefore, the abuser convinces the abused that no one but him loves her. In order to deserve his love, she must also accept his abuse. The weapon used here is fear; the victim fears not being loved. Therefore, they would rather have a false sense of love than to have no love at all. The use of fear in this way is evil.

The truth is real love does not ever seek to hurt. The Bible teaches that real love is patient, kind, not harsh, not fearful, or selfish, not ugly, or evil. Real love bears all things, real love builds up the other person, and it does not tear them down or try to destroy their very soul. Real love does not purposefully cause physical or emotional pain. I heard so many stories of a man telling a woman that he loves her just moments after he has beaten her physically or abused her emotionally. The problem is that this is not what love does. In summary, people in an abusive relationship stay because they believe in their own heart that the abuser loves them and no one else will.

HUMAN NEED: I NEED TO FEEL IMPORTANT.

This appears to be a favorite among abusers. I don't know how many times abused women have said to me, "But he needs me." Abusers tell their victims "I need you." This makes us feel important, the idea of being needed makes us feel wanted as well. But to purposefully hurt someone physically is an abuse of an important emotion. Many women keep returning to abusive relationships because they are convinced they are important to their abuser. But the truth is that the people that you are really important to you do not purposefully hurt you, instead, they purposefully nurture you. So, the summation of this is that abused women are convinced that their abuser needs them, and they need their abuser.

HUMAN NEED: I WANT HOPE.

This seems to be an area where the abuser really obtains control of the abused. Always promising things will change, things will become better, and "I won't do it again, I promise" are frequent terms of negotiation causing the abused to believe that things will change because they remain hopeful that the situation will improve. However, the reality is, without a genuine change of heart, the circumstances will not improve.

Another form of misusing this human need is the abuser convincing the abused that they are the one to blame. If they had the meal ready on time, if they had said the right thing, or worn the right clothing, things would have been different, they would not have hit you. Let me say here again, if you are being physically or emotionally abused, IT IS NOT YOUR FAULT! Abused people stay in abusive relationships because deep in their heart they are hopeful that circumstances will positively change. In these situations, the victim is always telling others, "it's not his fault, he doesn't mean it, he is sorry." The Bible tells us, *"Hope deferred maketh the heart sick . . . "* (Proverbs 13:12).

Another point worthy of mention here is denial. The need for hope is such a strong emotion that people will deny their own reality. They deny that they are being abused; they deny that the person abusing them would ever hurt them. In order to make any kind of progress in life, we must face our reality.

HUMAN NEED: I WANT TO LIVE! OR I WANT MY LIFE TO HAVE PURPOSE!

The abuser often uses this as a weapon against his victim, especially if children are involved. Threats are made by the abuser that they could take the children, or that without them they would have no reason to live. Often the abuser will threaten the victim with physical death, "If you leave me, I will hunt you down and kill you." This is tragic, but it does happen. The abused literally fears for their life.

Another way the abuser uses this human need in a demented way is that he threatens to commit suicide, often telling his victim that if he does so it will be the victim that actually will be killing them. In many cases, the abused victim reasons that this is a normal way of life. If a person grew up in an abusive home, then abuse is what they are familiar with, and we are secure in what we are familiar with, even if it slowly breaks us.

The final thought I wish to share in answer to the question is "why do I stay" because of the lack of resources or not believing that help is available. I assure you help is available! You can get out! The abuser provides a false sense of purpose in life.

QUESTION: WILL GOD DEAL WITH THE PERSON THAT HAS HURT ME?

The answer is yes! However, I cannot tell you the specifics of how or when. Some of that will be determined by weather or not the person who has hurt you seeks forgiveness themselves. And God's plans for our lives in these matters are entirely up to him. If you will recall from our chapter on forgiveness this is why the Apostle Paul said, concerning Alexander, "... *The Lord reward him according to his works*" (2 Timothy 4:14). This is why it is important to turn vengeance over to the Lord, but we can rest assured that God will do what he deems to be right.

We want to remember, for our own benefit, that God is both merciful and just. Justice is us receiving what we deserve, and mercy is us not attaining what we deserve. However, I will tell you what the Bible says about certain abuse.

Concerning causing harm to a child, Jesus Christ said, *"It were better for him that a millstone were hanged about his neck, and he cast into the sea, than that he should offend one of these little ones"* (Luke 17:2).

One way I believe God deals with people is by vexing them. The word vexed is used several times in Scripture; it means to irritate, to torment, to trouble, to afflict. A lot of people in the world are troubled or tormented because of the evil they have committed, perhaps this is one of the ways God deals with them for their evil acts. I realize that this is not a clear answer, and I really can't supply a clear answer except to say that God does not let evil go un-noticed, and He will ultimately deal with it.

QUESTION: WILL THE PERSON WHO HURT ME BE IN HEAVEN?

We cannot know another person's heart outside of their actions and behavior. The only way any of us will be in Heaven is if we have believed in Jesus Christ as our Saviour and confessed our sins and need of His Salvation. But if they have truly received Christ, their heart will be different, and their behavior will improve as well. The answer is yes, if the person who has hurt you receives Jesus Christ as Saviour they will be in Heaven. However, your relationship with them will be different in Heaven; they will be different, and you will be different. Heaven will be a sinless environment; evil will not be present. God will wipe all tears from our eyes, and we will not even remember the evil that was done to us.

QUESTION: HOW DO I HANDLE RELATIONSHIPS NOW?

Several important thoughts come to mind concerning this. First of all, you must guard your heart. One of the largest challenges an abused person has is trust. So, the key factor for you developing a good relationship with new people is providing them with the opportunity to earn your trust. Some might need to be aware of the fact that you have been hurt but how much they need to know must be determined by you. I would suggest only sharing with people with whom you develop a close relationship. The point is they need to know that you don't trust people quickly and that trust must be earned.

The next key then is that you must entrust them with the opportunity to earn your trust, and you must keep in mind that this is not the person that has abused you. The reality is everyone hurts us, and we hurt other people but usually not intentionally. But this person that is willing to earn your trust is not the person that abused you. This could be the exact person that God has sent to help you heal; this could be one of the people that will love you and treat you like the treasure that you are.

I do not encourage you to seek a relationship for the sake of having a relationship. True, we need relationships, we need to be loved, and we need companionship. But wait until you are strong and don't move too fast into making commitments to someone that has not proven themselves to you and has not yet earned your complete trust.

Now for a little pastoral advice, carefully choose a spiritual mentor. A person that is a strong Christian that will pray for you, help you guard your heart, and will watch out for your best interest. Once you have chosen a spiritual mentor, and you are confident that God has sent them to you, then listen to their advice and take heed to what they suggest to you. Granted, sometimes it is hard to find someone like this, but if you pray for such a person you will see that God is able to send someone to you. (More information is provided on this in the lesson on Trust).

QUESTION: SHOULD I TELL MY FUTURE SPOUSE?

On this question as with all of the questions, I sought input from my team of advisors on this project, all of whom have suffered abuse. The following is what we concluded. Yes, share some things with your future spouse; I would not offer details, but they need to know that because you have been abused you will have triggers and those triggers can be set off unexpectedly at times that might cause you to need to explain your actions. So, if you feel the need to be 100% transparent than do so. Leave everything with God, but if you feel comfortable sharing with others that you trust, do so.

QUESTION: WILL I SURVIVE IT ALL?

The past cannot be changed, but as we shared in the lesson entitled "Past – Present – Future, What I Can Change," you can change the way you view your past. By developing your relationship with Jesus Christ and following Biblical principles you can live a productive life. We sometimes have a wrong perspective about life. Psychology seems to tell us we cannot overcome experiences that have happened in our past, and some philosophies teach that we will never get over the past. These things are not the root issue. The issue is found in the question can I live in this moment in spite of terrible things that have taken place in my life? And the answer to that is yes, you can. Yes, you will survive! In Jesus Christ we have hope, we have value, and we are loved unconditionally.

QUESTION: WHAT DO I DO NOW?

This is perhaps one of the most important questions of all because we cannot change our past, we are in the present, and we can build a productive and victorious life for our future. So, I make these suggestions with the prayer that the principles shared in this book will be of help in your life journey. Draw close to the Lord Jesus Christ, and develop trust in your relationship with Him. He is the one that is able to heal your broken heart and bind up your wounds. Follow the Biblical principles in this book of forgiveness by making positive changes and letting God take your life back for you. Then I would encourage you to make plans, set goals, and take one step at a time toward the goals you set.

You can overcome!

You are loved!

You have value!

You can have good relationships!

You can live a victorious life!

PERSONAL REFLECTIONS

I would like to ask God:

_____

_____

_____

_____

I will pray, search the Scriptures, and ask God to answer in my heart. I will accept His answer whatever it may be, knowing that He loves me unconditionally.

CHAPTER SEVEN
TRUST

TRUST IS DEFINED IN THE dictionary as "confidence; a reliance or resting of the mind on the integrity, veracity, justice, friendship or other sound principle of another person." When a person has been abused, one of the many characteristics that abuse affects is the person's ability to trust. Anyone who has been abused, hurt, broken, betrayed, or wounded will discover it is difficult to trust people, and trust is something that cannot be restored with a pill. If an adult takes away your "teddy bear", then your level of trust in all adults is tarnished, and you will find it difficult to trust most adults from that day forward, unless trust is re-established in some way. My goal in this lesson is to establish Biblical principles for coming to terms with trust issues.

Trust is an important part of any relationship. When we are confident that we can trust the people closest to us, then we have much more confidence in ourselves. The most important factor in any relationship is trust. This goes all the way back to the beginning of time. When God placed Adam and Eve in the Garden of Eden, He gave them everything necessary to form a good relationship with Him and with each other. But as we know, Satan entered into the perfect relationship, and, having taken on the form of a snake, he attacked the woman's trust in God. Notice how this event is recorded in Scripture:

> *Now the serpent was more subtil than any beast of the field which the LORD God had made. And he said unto the woman, <u>Yea, hath God said</u>, Ye shall not eat of every tree of the garden? And the woman said unto the serpent, We may eat of the fruit of the trees of the garden: But of the fruit of the tree which is in the midst of the garden, God hath said, Ye shall not eat of it, neither shall ye touch it, lest ye die. And the serpent said unto the woman, Ye*

shall not surely die: For God doth know that in the day ye eat thereof, then your eyes shall be opened, and ye shall be as gods, knowing good and evil.
(Genesis 3:1-5, emphasis mine)

Notice the underlined portion in verse one where the Serpent (Satan) says, *"Yea, hath God said . . . "* Satan's objective here is to convince the woman to doubt what God had told her and Adam in order to break her trust in God and His Word. Later, God questioned Adam and Eve concerning what happened (of course He knew what happened because He is God). Eve answered, *"The Serpent beguiled me."* Sadly the word beguiled defines the behavior of abuse; it means "to deceive; to impose on by artifice or craft, by amusement." In other words, Satan found it amusing to break the trust between Eve and God.

Satan abused the first woman emotionally, and he caused her to question her trust in God. From that time until now, Satan has made abuse a favorite pass time of his. We know the history of what happened and the important point to be made here is that one of the core characteristics affected by abuse of any kind is broken trust, beginning with broken trust in God. So how can trust be re-established? How can we trust again? How do we know who to trust?

RE-ESTABLISH TRUST IN GOD

Early in life we receive our view of God from the prominent male in our lives. If this person is abusive to us, then our view of God is tarnished at the beginning of life. Then if we have been abused, we often ask ourselves why God allowed the abuse. We have attempted to answer this question with the fact that Satan is always at the center of abuse and has been from the beginning of time.

Remember, in the Garden of Eden Satan attacked the woman's trust in God and His Word. Even now Satan, "The Serpent" will do everything in his power to keep you from trusting God and His Word (The Bible) because Satan knows that God and His Bible are the very sources of healing and restoration to guide you onto the path of living and loving again. Satan and his demons will tell you that God does not love you, that God cannot be trusted, and that the Bible is not true.

Yet throughout the Bible, we find that God always came to those who were hurting, and He always offered hope, peace, and emotional healing through His only begotten Son Jesus Christ. Notice just a few of the events recorded in Scripture where Jesus Christ showed up to help.

- Jesus Christ was given to the World because you and I need a Saviour (John 3:16).
- Jesus stopped to heal the leper who no one else would even touch because of the disease of leprosy (Matthew 8:1-3).
- Jesus came to the Demoniac of Gadera who lived among the tombs (the dead) and was possessed and troubled by demons, cutting himself with stones. Everyone feared him, and no one could contain him. But Jesus showed up and cast out the demons and the man was at peace and *"in his right mind"* (Mark 5:1-20).
- When the Disciples were alone in a ship during a dangerous storm in fear for their lives, the Lord Jesus Christ walked on water to reach where they were on the sea. He calmed the storm and climbed into the ship with them (Matthew 14:22-36).
- Jesus came to the Samaritan woman at the well. She was broken, lonely and in need of forgiveness, peace, hope, and spiritual healing. The Lord Jesus Christ satisfied the thirst of her soul, and He can do the same for you (John 4:6-30).

These are only a few of many. You will also find, at the back of this book, testimonies of people whose lives Jesus Christ has transformed.

I realize that if you have been abused, then trusting anyone, even God, is difficult, but I encourage you to read on and consider trusting Him. If you already trust God, then I encourage you to trust Him more.

GOD'S HEALING HAND

It is against God's nature to hurt anyone, as a matter of fact, even for God to bring judgment and punishment upon the wicked is referred to in Scripture as *"... his strange work"* (Isaiah 28:21). In other words, it is against God's nature to even punish people who are deserving of punishment. God is love, God is life, God is grace, God is mercy, God is peace, and God is hope. All of these attributes and many more are manifested in the person of His only begotten Son Jesus Christ, who proclaimed at the beginning of His earthly ministry,

The Spirit of the Lord is upon me, because he hath anointed me to preach the gospel to the poor; he hath sent me to heal the brokenhearted, to preach deliverance to the captives, and recovering of sight to the blind, to set at liberty them that are bruised, To preach the acceptable year of the Lord. (Luke 4:18-19)

We see in the words of Jesus Christ that He is the healer of the broken and wounded. He binds-up those that Satan has wounded, and He heals the hearts of those that have been broken by Satan's evil works.

We can trace this truth all the way back to the beginning of mankind. When the first man and woman were attacked by Satan in the Garden of Eden, it was the voice of the Lord God (which most believe was Jesus Christ before He was born in Bethlehem) that came to them, made a sacrifice, and covered them with coats of skins.

God did not hurt you, it was not God that abused you, broke your heart, wounded your spirit, or invaded the temple of your body. God can be trusted because over two thousand years ago He sent His only begotten Son to heal the broken hearted, deliver the captive, and set at liberty them that are bruised, crushed, hurt, or broken.

HOW TO TRUST AGAIN

Trust is a synonym for faith. Throughout the Bible there are examples of God proving Himself to people in order to strengthen their faith in Him. As a matter of fact, if anyone has ever worked to earn our trust it is God. Moses is a good example for us to consider because not only did God earn Moses' trust (faith), but God also worked to develop Moses trust and confidence in his own abilities.

When God called out to Moses from the burning bush, He told Moses to take off his shoes because He was standing on Holy ground. Establishing that

He was God, that He had authority, and was already worthy of Moses reverence and trust. Then God introduced Himself to Moses further establishing that He was worthy of trust. *"Moreover he said, I am the God of thy father, the God of Abraham, the God of Isaac, and the God of Jacob. And Moses hid his face; for he was afraid to look upon God"* (Exodus 3:6). God establishes that Moses could trust Him because of the history of His trustworthiness. Abraham, Isaac, and Jacob were all men that Moses was familiar with. They had all trusted God, and He had delivered them and had done great deeds in their lives.

Pause and think about people you know for a moment. I certainly don't know you personally, and I do not know your specific circumstances. However, I'm certain that you know someone who is living the victorious Christian life. The challenge is that you have told yourself you could never live that kind of life. But you can! You can trust God just as they have and just as they do. We must all trust God a little today and a little more tomorrow. God has established that He is trustworthy through the lives of those who already trust Him and through the lives of those God has already delivered, emotionally healed, and transformed. Moses took a step of faith by trusting God because he knew the history of Abraham, Isaac, and Jacob, and he knew that God did not fail them. You can also take that step of faith because you can find people who have trusted Him, and He proved Himself trustworthy.

God shared His Concern with Moses,

And the LORD said, I have surely seen the affliction of my people which are in Egypt, and have heard their cry by reason of their taskmasters; for I know their sorrows; And I am come down to deliver them out of the hand of the Egyptians, and to bring them up out of that land unto a good land and a large, unto a land flowing with milk and honey; unto the place of the Canaanites, and the Hittites, and the Amorites, and the Perizzites, and the Hivites, and the Jebusites. (Exodus 3:7-8)

This is such a powerful truth, Notice the statement in verse seven, *"I know their sorrows."* You can trust again because God knows your sorrows, He is concerned, and He has the power, desire, and compassion to help.

God told Moses, *"Come now therefore, and I will send thee unto Pharaoh, that thou mayest bring forth my people the children of Israel out of Egypt"* (Exodus 3:10). God's plan was to send Moses to deliver the people from bondage. As mentioned earlier, I do not know your personal circumstances, but take a moment and look at your life right now. Has God sent someone to you? We know that He sent His Son Jesus Christ to deliver us. If you will look closely around you, perhaps you will see that God has also sent people to you, people to help you live and love again.

God helped Moses Trust Him gradually:

> And Moses answered and said, But, behold, they will not believe me, nor hearken unto my voice: for they will say, The LORD hath not appeared unto thee. And the LORD said unto him, What is that in thine hand? And he said, A rod. And he said, Cast it on the ground. And he cast it on the ground, and it became a serpent; and Moses fled from before it. And the LORD said unto Moses, Put forth thine hand, and take it by the tail. And he put forth his hand, and caught it, and it became a rod in his hand: That they may believe that the LORD God of their fathers, the God of Abraham, the God of Isaac, and the God of Jacob, hath appeared unto thee. (Exodus 4:1-5)

For Moses to cast his Shepherd's Rod on the ground was a small act of trust (faith). But Moses did so, and upon this act of trust, God proved Himself trustworthy. What do you have in your hand? I don't mean literally, I mean what are you holding in your hands that you could trust God with? Whatever it is, trust Him with that! You can trust Him gradually, He will prove Himself! God invites us, *"prove me now herewith, saith the LORD of hosts"* (Malachi 3:10).

WHO TO TRUST

This is the most challenging question on the issue of trust, especially for those who have been abused and are now looking for a romantic relationship. Here are several suggestions that you should find helpful.

TRUST PEOPLE WHO HAVE A GOOD RELATIONSHIP WITH GOD

Our relationship with God is the most important relationship in our lives. When a person is careful about their relationship with God, when they want it to be in good standing in God's fellowship, then they will have a desire for all other close relationships in their life to be in good standing also.

The common bond among Christians is the person of Jesus Christ. He is our common bond. When two people that believe in Jesus Christ are faithful in following Him, then they will share that common bond through the Holy Spirit, which creates a stronger relationship.

DON'T TRUST PEOPLE WITH A HISTORY OF BAD RELATIONSHIPS

When you encounter someone that complains or speaks negatively of all their relationships, insinuating that all of their relationships were bad, it is possible that they are the one with the problem. It could be that they do not know how to treat people. Of course, there could be good reason for this, but the point is if their entire relationship history is negative and toxic, don't expect it to be different with you if they have not tried to improve themselves. If they have not learned from the past, if they are blaming everyone else and not taking responsibility for their own behavior, chances are they are toxic. Stay away!

TRUST PEOPLE WHO RESPECT THEMSELVES

How well do they value themselves? Do they take care of their general appearance? Do they have a good work ethic? Do they take care of their personal belongings? Chances are high that if they do not respect themselves, then they will not respect you either.

TRUST PEOPLE WHO TREAT THEIR FAMILY MEMBERS WELL

Years ago, I was imparted with the advice that if a young lady treats her father well, then she will most likely treat her husband well. Certainly, we all have family challenges, but overall it is a pretty good measure that if a person speaks well of his family and he treats them well, then he will treat others well.

TRUST PEOPLE WHO TREAT PEOPLE WELL, ESPECIALLY THE PEOPLE THEY DON'T NEED

My friend Jimmy Barrett said, "You can judge a man's character by the way he treats people he doesn't need." This is a great truth about people. The person that is kind to the "least" among us is going to be the best among us and will be the kind of person that can be trusted in a relationship.

CHOOSE A SPIRITUAL MENTOR

We mentioned this in "Questions from the Heart, Answers from God," but let me emphasize the importance of a mentor here. My advice would be that you choose a dedicated Christian, one that sincerely cares about you, is willing to disciple you in the Christian faith, and will help you in decision making not only by sharing their opinions with you but taking the time to help you think through your decisions by showing you principles from the Bible and will faithfully pray for you.

If you are a lady, I would suggest that you choose a married couple that will work with you together. It is wise for a lady to choose a couple to mentor her because then she can gain another perspective. A wise mentor will encourage you to think things through, so as not to repeat bad decisions. It often comes down to have people in your life that help you guard your heart; keep your eyes on the prize, and to be a positive influence in your life. The best place to find spiritual mentors is in a Bible believing church. By this, I'm referring to a church that is centered on Jesus Christ and the Bible is used as the source for teaching and practice. A "church" that is all about emotion, feelings, prosperity, wealth and partying will not meet your true spiritual and emotional needs. A Bible believing church is one that seeks solutions for life's challenges from the Bible and leads people to a relationship with Jesus Christ and helps them develop that relationship.

The way to make the most of a spiritual mentor is to go to them for advice and take their advice to heart. If you are still struggling with issues in your life, then I highly suggest that you not make any major decisions in life, especially relationship decisions, without seeking the counsel of your spiritual mentor. When your mentor provides his or her perspective, then take his or her advice into account when making your decisions.

One of the best spiritual mentors God provides us with is a caring pastor. We find this important truth in Scripture: *"Remember them which have the rule over you, who have spoken unto you the word of God: whose faith follow, considering the end of their conversation"* (Hebrews 13:7). This principle applies to any spiritual mentor, the person or people, who speak the Bible to you, and pray for you, follow their faith, consider the point of their conversation. Hebrews 13:17 says, *"Obey them that have the rule over you, and submit yourselves: for they watch for your souls, as they that must give account, that they may do it with joy, and not with grief: for that is unprofitable for you."* The statement *"for they watch for your souls"* is the key to a good spiritual mentor.

The person who is truly watching for your soul is the one that will go the distance with you. They will seek to lead you in the best path, will help you make the best decisions, will base their counsel on Biblical truths and will help you guard your heart in all relationships.

PERSONAL REFLECTIONS

I will work by establishing or re-establishing trust in God by:

_____

_____

_____

_____

I'm going to strengthen my trust in God by asking Him to help me with the following:

_____

_____

_____

_____

I see _____ as a person God has placed into my life that I can trust.

My spiritual mentor is: _____.

CHAPTER EIGHT
CONFRONTING GIANTS

MOST OF US ARE FAMILIAR with the history of David and Goliath found in 1 Samuel 17 of the Bible. In the valley of Elah, the giant Goliath stood defying the armies of Israel, cursing the name of God, and challenging Saul and his army for a fight to the finish to determine which nation would serve the other. King Saul and his army feared the giant and the army of the Philistines and for forty days no man in Saul's army was brave enough to confront the giant Goliath.

On the fortieth day of the battle, the young shepherd boy and future king of Israel came to the valley of Elah bringing food for his brothers and those serving in the army with them. When David arrived, he heard the vulgarity of Goliath and the challenge set by the Giant. David also witnessed the fear of Saul and his army and determined in his own heart to confront the Giant and destroy him.

From this event, we see important and powerful principles about confronting the giants in our lives. We know from Scripture the way it all ended. David confronted Goliath with a slingshot and five smooth stones, and with God's help, he took the giant down and took off his head. We are going to take a journey through the events that led to Goliath's defeat and learn biblical principles that you can apply to your own life, which will enable you to confront your giants and continue your life journey of living and loving again.

KNOW THE HEART OF THE BATTLE

Over the years, I have heard some remarkable sermons and Bible lessons on the Slaying of Goliath by the shepherd boy David, but, in all honesty, I don't recall ever hearing anyone state clearly what the battle was over, except to point out that Goliath was cursing the name of the living God. We find that the purpose for the heart of the battle is given clearly in verses eight and nine:

And he stood and cried (spoke loudly) unto the armies of Israel, and said unto them, Why are ye come out to set your battle in array? Am not I a Philistine, and ye servants to Saul? Choose you a man for you, and let him come down to me. <u>If he be able to fight with me, and to kill me, then will we be your servants: but if I prevail against him, and kill him, then shall ye be our servants, and serve us.</u> (1 Samuel 17:8-9, emphasis mine)

I have underlined verse nine, which clearly provides us with the answer to what was at stake and what the real heart of the battle was over. If Goliath and his army defeated the army of Israel, then the Israelites would serve the Philistines and would be in bondage to them. But, if Saul's army could kill Goliath and defeat the army of the Philistines, then the Philistines would be in bondage to Israel. So, it comes down to this, the battle was over who was going to be in control of who. To use our "teddy bear" analogy, the battle was over who was going to have possession and control of the teddy bear.

Although everyone has different circumstances, let's consider what we can learn from the principle of who has possession and who is in control. Do the events of the past possess and control you? Do the people who hurt you in the past possess and control your present-day thoughts? Do the emotions of anger, hate, fear, bitterness, malice, depression, and vengeance control your life? Do the giants in your life have dominion over your thoughts, your emotions, your dreams, your self-value, and your hopes? If they do, then this is the heart of the battle in your life. Who do you serve and who serves you? Who or what are you in bondage to?

We must confront your giants. You must come to terms with the giants that are trying to conquer you. Those giants can be defeated, they can be brought down, and their heads can be removed! With God's help you can do it. You can choose whom you serve, and you can choose whom you will relinquish control of your life to. You can confront your giants. You can conquer them, and you can live and love again.

PARALYZED BY FEAR

The battle in the Valley of Elah between Saul's army and the Philistines had gone on for forty days. Everyday Goliath stood in the face of Saul's army and challenged them, *"... choose you a man for you, and let him come down to me. If he be able to fight with me, and to kill me, then will we be your servants: but if I prevail against him, and kill him, then shall ye be our servants, and serve us."*

We find the response of Saul and his army in verse eleven, *"When Saul and all Israel heard those words of the Philistine, they were dismayed, and greatly afraid."* There are two words here that clearly reveal why Saul's army did not accept Goliaths challenge, and their lack of confronting the giant is what kept them servants to Goliath while the battle raged on. The first word to notice is "dismayed", which means to be "disheartened, deprived of courage." This is a sad place to be in, to have lost heart, to have relinquished hope, but this is the perspective that Saul and his army had in the valley of Elah.

Sadly, many people who struggle to overcome the tragic events of the past view their lives in the same way. They are disheartened and greatly afraid. The purpose of this book is to encourage you with Biblical truths so that you might find the courage to confront your giants.

The second word to take note of is the word "afraid" or "fear." Saul's army was not only afraid, but they were *"greatly afraid."* Fear is defined as "a painful emotion or passion excited by an expectation of evil, or the apprehension of impending danger." So, Saul and his army did not accept Goliaths challenge because they were afraid of defeat, instead of expecting victory over Goliath and the Philistine army. When we approach our giants biblically, we can expect victory. That does not mean we will not be afraid, but it does mean we can confront our giants with courage.

DAVID CONFRONTED HIS FEARS

In preparing this chapter, I consulted with my team and asked what fears or "giants" an abused person would most likely have to confront, the following is a list comprised by them. We will not specifically deal with them individually, however, what we will offer are Biblical principles that will help you confront your "giants."

GIANTS BY NAME

We have listed these giants in the form of questions so can evaluate from your own heart if any of them are giants you need to confront.

- Do I worry about someone finding out what has happened to me?
- Do I worry about being embarrassed by others knowing my pain?
- Am I hurting in silence?
- Am I afraid of trusting again?
- Am I struggling with depression?
- Will I ever be loved?
- Are my thoughts ever going to be better than they are right now?
- Will I be able to have children?
- Will I be able to serve God?
- How will people react to me and act toward me?
- Will I ever be good enough?
- Will I ever measure up?

These are not easy giants to confront, but I want to encourage you that the giants can be confronted, they can be conquered, and they can be slain! Before David walked out onto the battlefield with his slingshot in hand to confront the giant Goliath, he had already confronted his own fears. We see this in David's words to King Saul in 1 Samuel 17:32-36:

> And David said to Saul, Let no man's heart fail because of him; thy servant will go and fight with this Philistine. And Saul said to David, Thou art not able to go against this Philistine to fight with him: for thou art but a youth,

and he a man of war from his youth. And David said unto Saul, Thy servant kept his father's sheep, and there came a lion, and a bear, and took a lamb out of the flock: And I went out after him, and smote him, and delivered it out of his mouth: and when he arose against me, I caught him by his beard, and smote him, and slew him. Thy servant slew both the lion and the bear . . .

David informs Saul that he has had victory over other adversaries and was willing to confront the Giant Goliath. The important point to understand is that before David ever confronted the lion and the bear, he had to confront his own fear of the lion and the bear, and he had to find the courage to confront them. Where could this courage have come from?

First of all, it is important for us to know that when David killed the lion and the bear he was a shepherd caring for his father's sheep. Here is where we make this truth personal for our own lives. David found the courage to confront the lion and the bear out of the love he had for his father and his father's sheep. He overcame his fear out of his responsibility for protecting his father's sheep. David overcame his fear of the lion to rescue only one lamb.

How does this situation apply to your life? Consider the value of your own life, consider that you have a heavenly Father that loves you and you certainly have friends that love you and care about you, and they don't enjoy the fact that you have been hurt and that your life is being controlled by an enemy and that you are in bondage to whatever and whoever your giants are. Let your courage to confront the giants in your life come from a love for living and loving again, and overcome your fear by focusing your faith in the Lord Jesus Christ, His strength, His love for you, and His willingness to confront your giants with you. You are the one lamb that is worthy of being rescued from the lion, so confront your fears.

RULES OF ENGAGEMENT

Until David arrived in the Valley of Elah, Goliath had set the rules of engagement, which defines the circumstances, conditions, degree, and manner in which the use of force or actions may be applied. It was Goliath that told Saul's army to choose a man to fight him and that the loser would be servant to the victor. But when David arrived at the Valley of Elah, he set his own rules of engagement.

David's first term of engagement was that he would go and fight the giant himself, as he declared in 1 Samuel 17:32, *"And David said to Saul, Let no man's heart fail because of him; <u>thy servant will go and fight with this Philistine</u>."* David determined that he would not allow Goliath to go unchallenged so he decided that he would confront the giant himself. Not only was this a rule of engagement made on David's part, but it was an important decision. Like David, you must decide that you will confront the giants in your life. You must make fighting your giant one of your rules of engagement.

David's second rule of engagement is found in verse thirty-seven, *"David said moreover, <u>The LORD</u> that delivered me out of the paw of the lion, and out of the paw of the bear, <u>he will deliver me out of the hand of this Philistine</u>. And Saul said unto David, Go, and the LORD be with thee"* (1 Samuel 17:37). David's rule of engagement was that he would confront the Giant with the help of God.

David's third condition of battle was that he would choose his own weapons. We see this in verses 38-40:

> *And Saul armed David with his armour, and he put an helmet of brass upon his head; also he armed him with a coat of mail (coat of steel). And David girded his sword upon his armour, and he assayed to go; for he had not proved it. And David said unto Saul, I cannot go with these; for I have not proved them. And David put them off him. And he took his staff in his hand, and chose him five smooth stones out of the brook, and put them in a shepherd's bag which he had, even in a scrip; and his sling was in his hand: and he drew near to the Philistine.*

David attempted to wear the armor of the army of Israel, but David was not even a grown man, he was not a soldier, he was a shepherd boy, and Saul's armor did not fit him and would not work for him. Another important point is that Saul's armor was the same as the armor Goliath was using. Goliath had armor, and Saul's army had armor. Goliath had a helmet, and Saul's army had helmets. Goliath had a sword, and Saul's army had swords. Yet none of the soldiers in Saul's army were able to confront the giant Goliath. So here is an important principle for us; the enemies' weapons may not work against the enemy.

The weapons the giant in your life has used against you, may not work to defeat him. If your giant has used hatred, anger, bitterness, perversion, vengeance, manipulation, and malice against you, then it is unlikely that those same weapons will work against him. David did not go out to confront Goliath with the same armor and weapons the giant had. David went out to confront the giant with his shepherd's staff, his slingshot, and five smooth stones. Not the weapons of a giant, but the tools of a shepherd.

As you go forth to confront your giant, choose your weapons carefully. The weapons of truth, forgiveness, love, confidence, faith in the promises of God, and a determination to be free from the bondage and control of the giant are the greatest weapons against evil.

THE BEST PROVEN WEAPON

When David put Saul's armor and sword on, he then attempted to go with them but quickly realized that he had not proven the armor and sword, *"... And David said unto Saul, I cannot go with these; for I have not proven them."* David had not tried or experienced the armor and weapon Saul had suggested. Since David already had his shepherds staff and slingshot he went to the brook and found five smooth stones. David had proven these things, and he had experienced victory with his Shepherd's staff and slingshot, and he knew they would work because they had been tried and tested.

The most proven weapon of all is the Word of God (The Bible). It has been tried and it has withstood the tests of time. Perhaps you have never considered the Bible as a weapon, but the Bible refers to itself as a weapon, Hebrews 4:12 tells us, *"For the word of God is quick, and powerful, and sharper than any twoedged sword, piercing even to the dividing asunder of soul and spirit, and of the joints and marrow, and is a discerner of the thoughts and intents of the heart."*

I want to encourage you that the principles shared in this book are Biblical; they are principles that have been tried, tested, and proven. Take them to heart, grant them a chance, and apply them to your own life and circumstances and you will find that they are quick (living), powerful, and sharper than any two-edged sword. They have been tested through the ages and been proven to help people in the trials of life, the worst of circumstances, and in all walks of life. The Bible has enabled thousands of people to confront and defeat their giants. Open your heart and give Gods Word a chance to help you confront and defeat your giants! Thousands have proven that the Bible does work!

"... PUT THEM OFF..."

After David put Saul's armor and sword on, he realized they would not work for him, as verse thirty-nine states, *"And David put them (Saul's armor and sword) off him."* The point is that sometimes we are unable to defeat our giants because we are fighting with the wrong weapons. For David, Saul's Helmet of Brass, Coat of Mail, and Sword would not work, so he "put them off." Just as we need to equip ourselves with the best armor and weaponry, we must also "put off" the weapons that are ineffective against our giants.

Paul tells us in Colossians 3:8 *"... put off all these; anger, wrath, malice, blasphemy, filthy communication out of your mouth."* You will never defeat your adversary with anger, wrath, bitterness, hatred, malice, manipulation, and vengeance. If these are the weapons you have tried and failed with in the past it is time to "put them off." The term put off literally means to cast away, to cast aside. Remove these emotions from your heart and take up the weapons that are effective.

PERSONAL REFLECTIONS

My greatest fear:

_____

_____

_____

_____

I can find the courage to overcome my fear because:

_____

_____

_____

_____

My terms of engagement for confronting my fears:

_____

_____

_____

_____

CHAPTER NINE
PREPARE FOR WARFARE

I REFER AGAIN TO 1 Samuel 17:40 for this extremely important point, *"And he (David) took his staff in his hand, and chose him five smooth stones out of the brook, and put them in a shepherd's bag which he had, even in a scrip; and his sling was in his hand: and he drew near to the Philistine."* I picture David walking to the brook with his Shepherd's staff in hand, kneeling down by the water's edge while he carefully sorts through the stones lying by the brook. He strategically chooses the five smooth stones, perhaps as he selects each stone he wipes any debris off in his hands and toss's them into the air, catches them in his hand, looks carefully at the selected stone, and places each one in his pouch. As he is selecting the stones he is praying, and, in his mind, he is contemplating every move, every word, and action he will execute when he is standing face to face with his adversary Goliath. David carefully took the time to prepare himself, physically, emotionally, and spiritually.

My friend, before you confront your giants, it is imperative that you prepare yourself physically, emotionally, and spiritually. The emotional and spiritual parts are the most important. Proverbs 24:6 admonishes us, *"For by wise counsel thou shalt make thy war: and in multitude of counsellors there is safety."* The word counsel means "deliberation or consultation." Before you confront the giants in your life, consult the biblical principles put forth in this book, pray for wisdom and guidance, and be sure you have a good spiritual and emotional support team. Prepare yourself spiritually to confront the giant.

THE GREATEST WEAPON OF ALL

As David stood before Goliath he said: *"Thou comest to me with a sword, and with a spear, and with a shield: but I come to thee in the name of the LORD of hosts, the God of the armies of Israel, whom thou hast defied"* (1 Samuel 17:45). David stood on the side of right, and he went out to confront the enemy in the name of the Lord of hosts. The reality is we do not have the power in ourselves to overcome evil. We do not have the power to take down the giants in our lives; we need the help and power of God. This power comes through prayer and through putting the Word of God in your heart. You don't have to confront your giants alone because you can confront them in the name of the LORD of hosts. In the name of Jesus Christ!

DAVID HAD THE ARMOR AND WEAPON, GOD HAD THE POWER

1 Samuel 17:49 says, *"And David put his hand in his bag, and took thence a stone, and slang it, and smote the Philistine in his forehead, that the stone sunk into his forehead; and he fell upon his face to the earth."* The stone from David's slingshot hit Goliath in the forehead, yet he fell forward on his face. Usually, when someone is hit in the forehead, the natural reaction is that they fall backwards. But with the right weapon in David's hand, the power of God caused the giant to fall forward. It was God that actually killed Goliath, but God would not do His part until someone was willing to confront the giant. The point is, God is able to defeat your giants, but you must be willing to confront them biblically, with a right attitude, right intentions, with the proper terms of engagement, and with the right weapons.

GOLIATH HAD FOUR BROTHERS

We recall that David chose five smooth stones before he went to confront the Giant Goliath. This was not because he thought it would take five stones to defeat Goliath; it was because Goliath had four brothers, and David was going to confront and defeat all of them. Your giant has other giants. Your greatest giant has other giants standing with him, battling over control in your life. The other giants might be your own emotions, your doubts, your low self-value, your regrets, or a number of other things. When Goliath fell to his death, the other giants, along with the entire Philistine army, fled. When you defeat the primary giant, the other ones will fall one by one, but they must all be confronted.

GOD KILLED GOLIATH, DAVID REMOVED HIS HEAD

1 Samuel 17:50-51 says:

So David prevailed over the Philistine with a sling and with a stone, and smote the Philistine, and slew him; but there was no sword in the hand of David. Therefore David ran, and stood upon the Philistine, and took his sword, and drew it out of the sheath thereof, and slew him, and cut off his head therewith.

And when the Philistines saw their champion was dead, they fled.

With Goliath's own sword David removed his head. This is symbolic and important. The word head is often used figuratively, referring to the person in authority, or the person that is in control. When David removed Goliath's head, he was presenting a clear message to the rest of the Philistine army that they were no longer in control of the battle, they had been defeated, and they would not control the people of Israel. David was also sending a message to Saul's army that Goliath and the Philistines would not have control over them because David confronted the giant Goliath; they were the victors.

Of course, you won't be physically removing anyone's head. However, by confronting your giants, even if you must confront them in your own mind, (which I believe David did while he was choosing the five smooth stones) you can remove the giant from having control in your thoughts, your emotions, and your future. Let God take the giant down, and then you remove his head.

Another application concerning David removing Goliath's head with his own sword is that in the end Goliath was destroyed by his own weapon. Goliath used the sword as a weapon of intimidation, hate, and destruction, and in the end Goliath died by the sword. The person that uses hate, anger, vengeance, bitterness, manipulation, and even perversion as weapons against their victims will be destroyed in the end by their own weapons, just as Goliath was.

CONFRONT YOUR GIANT, OTHERS WILL HELP

1 Samuel 17:52-53 tells us that after David had slain the giant and taken off his head that the men of Israel then fell in and pursued the Philistine army:

And the men of Israel and of Judah arose, and shouted, and pursued the Philistines, until thou come to the valley, and to the gates of Ekron. And the wounded of the Philistines fell down by the way to Shaaraim, even unto Gath, and unto Ekron. And the children of Israel returned from chasing after the Philistines, and they spoiled their tents.

We recall that this entire army including King Saul was afraid of the Giant Goliath, but once they saw that David had confronted the Giant they got involved to help, and they pursued the army of the Philistines.

There is a principle here, and it is this. We cannot expect people to fight all our battles for us, and sometimes we cannot expect people to support us until they see that we are willing to confront our giants. Until you are willing to muster the courage and the faith to confront your own giants you will find it a challenge for people to believe you are serious about victory in your life. But once you prove that you are willing to stand up to your giants, to confront them head on with sling-shot in hand, then you will find people will come to your aid, and they will help you run off the army that helped enable your giant. When you act, others will take action with you, when you stand others will stand with you, when you gather your five smooth stones for battle, others will support you, and when you go out to confront your giant, others will confront him with you!

There is one more thought to be added to this principle and that is one must realize you cannot depend on everyone to stand with you. The ones that will be the most willing and the most dependable will be other "Giant Slayers," people who have confronted and slain their own giants in life and people who make it their calling to help others confront their giants. So, in other words as you prepare to confront your Giants you want a "David type" of person to stand with you.

WHOSE CHILD ARE YOU?

After King Saul witnessed David's victory over the Giant he enquired as to whose son David was. In 1 Samuel 17:55-58 tells us:

> *And when Saul saw David go forth against the Philistine, he said unto Abner, the captain of the host, Abner, whose son is this youth? And Abner said, As thy soul liveth, O king, I cannot tell. And the king said, Enquire thou whose son the stripling is. And as David returned from the slaughter of the Philistine, Abner took him, and brought him before Saul with the head of the Philistine in his hand. And Saul said to him, Whose son art thou, thou young man? And David answered, I am the son of thy servant Jesse the Bethlehemite.*

The King was so impressed by David's courage, bravery and faith that he wanted to know whose son he was, who had raised such a brave warrior, who was this young man's father? Here is something for you to meditate on. If you are trusting in Jesus Christ as your Saviour, then you are a child of God. You are His, and He is yours, and God's children are all Giant slayers. So as any time you go forth to confront a Giant in your life, no matter how enormous, believe in your heart that Jesus Christ loves you and through your faith in Him, you are a child of God, and God's children are Giant Slayers.

Many times, in my mind I have pictured Abner going to David and inviting him to King Saul's tent. I can picture David following Abner into King Saul's tent dragging the head of Goliath with him, standing there in the presence of the King with Goliaths head in hand, Saul questions the young shepherd boy, *"Whose son art thou, thou young man?"* I can hear David humbly yet confidently answer, *"I am the son of thy servant Jesse."* My friend you can defeat the giants in your life because you are a child of God, you have it within your reach to be a Giant Slayer. When you confront your giants remember that you belong to someone, remember that you have a Heavenly Father that loves you and desires for you to be victorious!

OUR BIGGEST GIANT

The thought of David, the young shepherd boy standing before the nine-foot six-inch giant Goliath with his sling-shot and five smooth stones is certainly motivating and invigorating. The thought of David's victory over Goliath gives us the confidence to confront the giants in our own lives.

But there is a bigger giant that David confronted later on in his life that was perhaps more intimidating than Goliath. The giant I am referring to is David's own heart. In Psalm 139:23-24, David goes to God in prayer with an open heart and asks God to help him confront what is in his heart, *"Search me, O God, and know my heart: try me, and know my thoughts: And see if there be any wicked way in me, and lead me in the way everlasting."* This is the most challenging and most courageous thing any of us will ever do. To go humbly to God, open our own heart before Him and look deep inside of our own heart. Then once we have looked into our heart we must confront the giants that are there. Just as this would be our greatest of all challenges, it would also be our greatest of all victories. It is when we can slay the giants of fear, anger, vengeance, manipulation, hate, bitterness, and wrath that we will truly be the victors. And once we have confronted what is in our own hearts and conquered what is there that we will be able to conquer all other giants.

PERSONAL REFLECTIONS

My weapons for confronting my fears:

_____

_____

_____

_____

Those whom I trust to stand with me to help me confront my giants and help me to victory:

_____

_____

_____

_____

CHAPTER TEN
SELF-VALUE

WHAT IS YOUR VALUE? THIS is a different question than asking what you are worth. Financially, one could be worth over one million dollars but that does not determine a person's value. Another question that is asked of people is: how is your self-esteem? This is a psychological term having to do with how a person emotionally evaluates their own worth and what they believe about themselves. One of the challenges with self-esteem is that people often determine their own self-esteem by events that have taken place in their lives, what other people have convinced them about themselves, and their present circumstances. We are talking about something much more important when we refer to self-value.

In Matthew 13, Jesus Christ illustrated a great truth using a parable. A parable is a fable or story used to illustrate a moral truth. In Matthew 13:44-46, the Lord Jesus explains:

Again, the kingdom of heaven is like unto treasure hid in a field; the which when a man hath found, he hideth, and for joy thereof goeth and selleth all that he hath, and buyeth that field. Again, the kingdom of heaven is like unto a merchant man, seeking goodly pearls: Who, when he had found one pearl of great price (value), went and sold all that he had, and bought it.

The great Bible teacher, Arno C. Gaebelien said of this passage, "The parable of the treasure and the pearl go together. The man in both is not the sinner who seeks a treasure and a pearl, who gives up all in order to get all. The man is our Lord, who buys the field. He gave all he had to have the treasure (Israel) hid in the field. Who sold all to have the one pearl of great price (the church)!" I like Mr. Gaebelien's summary of the text. I like the idea of the Lord selling all to have one pearl of great price. I use this passage in Matthew's gospel to address our topic of self-value.

I refer again to the question: what is your value? The sad reality is that some people don't see any value in themselves; they don't believe anyone has ever wanted them and some believe they are not important to anyone. They have been beaten down, they have been abused and wounded, they have had setbacks in life, and they wonder in their hearts if anyone truly cares for them. They ask themselves if anyone really loves them and if you were to ask what is your self-value, if they were to answer what they believe in their heart, they would answer nothing. The Word of God describes how to truly measure your self-value. The Word of God reveals what your true value is.

THE GIFT OFFERED

John 3:16, the most famous verse in the Bible states, *"For God so loved the world that he gave his only begotten Son . . . "* The people that love us the most usually provide us with the highest gift they possibly can. For example, a loving grandmother may sacrifice her own personal needs to offer her grandchild, whom she loves unconditionally and values above many other people in her life, the most magnificent gifts that she can offer.

Think of the people you love the most. You are probably like the loving grandmother, and the people you cherish the most in life are those you probably make personal sacrifices for, so you are able to deliver the most valuable gifts to them. You make the sacrifices out of love, and you make the sacrifices, so you can grant fantastic gifts because you want the receiver to believe that you love them. God gave the most valuable gift to you out of love also. *"For God so loved . . . that he gave his only begotten Son . . . "* God wants you to believe that He loves you, and He wants you to believe that you are valuable to Him. To express His love for you and to express how valuable you truly are to Him; God gave the very best that He had, and He offered His most treasured possession so that He could purchase the one pearl of great price, which is you.

THE LIFE OFFERED

Jesus Christ proclaimed himself to be the giver of life, and He also proclaimed His ability to take back what the enemy has taken from you. In the Gospel of John, we read these words of Jesus, *"The thief (Satan) cometh not, but for to steal, and to kill, and to destroy: I am come that they might have life, and that they might have it more abundantly."* In these words, the Lord Jesus provides a clear account of how much He values you. He is willing to help you take back everything that the enemy has stolen, killed (deprived of life), and destroyed in your life. And then He offers to give life, but not only to give life but to give life more abundantly (overflowing). Jesus Christ offers life; He is the giver of life. He offers to give your life purpose because in His eyes, you are the treasure in the field; you are the pearl of great price.

Colossians 2:13-14 describes what Jesus Christ did for us on the Cross:

And you, being dead in your sins and the uncircumcision of your flesh, hath he quickened together with him, having forgiven you all trespasses; Blotting out the handwriting of ordinances that was against us, which was contrary to us, and took it out of the way, nailing it to his cross.

The reality that Jesus Christ willingly went to the Cross is perhaps the greatest measure of the value He sees in you. Jesus Christ saw so much value in you that He took all of your sin, all of those things that were against you, He took the punishment for you, and He nailed them to the Cross. You are so valuable that upon your confession He forgives you of past, present, and future sin. It was on the Cross that He gave His all to purchase the treasure that was in the field. It was on the Cross that He sold all that He had that He might purchase the one pearl of great price. Your self-value is not measured by how you see yourself or by how others value you. Your self-value was measured when Jesus Christ carried the Cross up the hill and gave His all to purchase your soul.

GOD'S INVOLVEMENT

Your value is measured by God's desire to be involved in your life. There are many passages of Scripture that confirms this point. In Matthew 6:26-30, we find the Lord Jesus stating Gods desire to be involved in our lives:

> *Behold the fowls of the air: for they sow not, neither do they reap, nor gather into barns; yet your heavenly Father feedeth them. Are ye not much better than they? Which of you by taking thought can add one cubit unto his stature? And why take ye thought for raiment? Consider the lilies of the field, how they grow; they toil not, neither do they spin: And yet I say unto you, That even Solomon in all his glory was not arrayed like one of these. Wherefore, if God so clothe the grass of the field, which today is, and tomorrow is cast into the oven, shall he not much more clothe you, O ye of little faith?*

God values us more than we can ever begin to imagine, He wants to be involved in our lives. He wants us to trust Him with our burdens, our dreams, and our daily needs. It is by us placing more and more of our trust in Him that we begin to realize the value that He sees in us.

GOD'S UNCONDITIONAL ACCEPTANCE

One of the most grievous emotions in life is that of not feeling accepted, not feeling wanted or loved. These feelings would certainly cause us to have a low self-value. The good news is that Scripture tells us in Ephesians 6:1 that we are accepted in God's love, *"To the praise of the glory of his grace, wherein he hath made us accepted in the beloved."* Of ourselves we are unworthy, but because God loves us and because Jesus Christ died on the Cross *". . . while we were yet sinners . . ."* our value is in the Lord Jesus Christ; we are accepted in Him as the beloved. And He accepts us as we are, like the man in Matthew 13 who sold all that he had to purchase the field for the treasure that was in the field. Not only did he obtain the treasure, but he also acquired all the debris that was in the field. He accepted the bad with the treasure. God knows that we have weaknesses. He knows that we have imperfections, scars, and even sin in our lives. But He looks beyond all of that and sees the treasure that is in us. And He accepts us as we are; believing we can become something more.

THE PRICE PAID

Years ago, I read a story about a tradition in a foreign land from long ago. The tradition was that when a young man was interested in a young lady for marriage he had to offer the young lady's father a cow. There was a certain poor man that had a daughter; she was attractive but not overly so. She was a nice young lady with a pleasant personality. A young man from a family of some means lived in the village and had an interest in the young lady. They were acquainted with each other. The young man had worked hard, made some business transactions, and saved up his resources for the purpose of asking the young lady's father for her hand in marriage. One day, the young man gathered up ten cows he had worked hard to collect. Keep in mind that he could have acquired the young lady's hand in marriage for one cow, but he worked hard to offer ten cows. Why? Because he wanted his bride to know that he saw her as being valuable, and he was willing to pay what he thought she was worth. Ten cows instead of one.

The point is that the value of something is often determined by the price that had been paid for it. Ephesians 1:7 says: *"In whom we have redemption through his blood, the forgiveness of sins, according to the riches of his grace."* The word redemption or redeem means to purchase back, to ransom, to liberate from captivity or bondage. You are very valuable to God. He paid the greatest price to redeem you, the innocent blood of His only begotten Son Jesus Christ was shed on the Cross, where He gave His life, and then three days later He arose from the grave. He sold all to purchase the field, and He sold all that He had to purchase the Pearl of Great Price, and you are that pearl.

You are extremely valuable, you were bought with a price, and the price was the innocent blood of Jesus Christ. He sold all to purchase your soul. Your self-value has nothing to do with where you came from, who your parents are, or how much money is or is not in your bank account. Your self-value has nothing to do with what others think about you or even what you think of yourself; your self-value rests in one truth and in one person. The person is Jesus Christ, and the truth is that He paid the ultimate price, so you would know that He loves you and, so you would not have to wonder, "Do I have any value?" Your self-value was determined by the price that was paid for your redemption and that was the life and shed blood of Jesus Christ.

"All that I needed to know about self-esteem or self-value I learned from a Sunday school teacher when I was five-years-old, a lady named

Georgia Parish, she taught me the words to a song that I still love to sing. 'Jesus loves me this I know, for the Bible tells me so.'"

—Don Woodard

PERSONAL REFLECTION

Based on what Jesus Christ has done for me I know that I have value because:

_____

_____

_____

_____

CHAPTER ELEVEN

WRITTEN ON YOUR HEART

IN 1986, DR. GUY DOUD was honored by President Ronald Reagan for Teacher of the Year. He was chosen from more than two million public school teachers. Dr. Doud has committed his life to motivating High School students to excellence. I received a video of an interview Dr. Doud gave, and my heart was blessed by a statement he made in the interview.

Dr. Doud is a committed Christian. In the interview, he said that because he taught in a public high school, he could not "Preach the Gospel" to his students, but that he could write on the tablets of their hearts. Dr. Doud found this principle in 2 Corinthians 3:2-3,

Ye are our epistle written in our hearts, known and read of all men: Forasmuch as ye are manifestly declared to be the epistle of Christ ministered by us, written not with ink, but with the Spirit of the living God; not in tables of stone, but in fleshy tables of the heart.

From this passage and some wonderful thoughts that Dr. Doud shared in his interview, there is a great principle of hope and healing.

Before we delve into the principle, let's begin by defining some of the words in the Scripture to help us have a better understanding of the principle. The first word is epistle, which means a writing directed or sent, a letter. The second is the phrase *"tables of stone."* This refers to a stone tablet used for writing on as they did in biblical times. Stone and leather were commonly used to write on then just as we use paper tablets and now we have electronic tablets. The third phrase in verse three is *"fleshy tables of the heart."* The key word here is fleshy, which simply means the soft part of the heart. The final and most important word in the passage is the word heart, and I want to be concise in the definition of what the heart is. Your heart is the very center of your being. It refers to the totality of an individual. It does not just speak of the emotions, nor does it just symbolize the mind, rather the heart refers to the center of one's personality. It is the very foundation of ones being, which includes the intellect, the emotions, and the will. When spoken of in the Bible, the heart refers to the total person.

In the passage, the Apostle Paul is referring to the idea that God had written the Old Covenant in stone, but the New Covenant was written on the heart of the believer for Jesus Christ by the Holy Spirit with the blood of Christ. Paul makes the point that the things *"written in our hearts are known and read by all men."* Now here is the principle: people in our lives write on the tablet of our heart, and we write on the hearts of others. Good and bad, we all have things written on our hearts. People who have been abused have had their heart written on and the negative things written become one of their struggles.

THE TABLET OF THE HEART

We have already defined what the heart is, and now we remind ourselves that the heart, the center of our being is the tablet that has been written on in our lives. We know that the heart is sometimes hard, life experiences can harden our hearts, and our emotions can become hard and calloused. And yet the heart can sometimes be soft, good things come our way, and blessings and special events in life can soften our heart. The heart is always fragile, but sometimes it is more fragile than other times. It is extremely fragile in our youth, and in times of depression and despair, the heart can be fragile. Of course, sometimes the heart is weak, and sometimes it is strong. Our heart is the tablet that is written on in life.

THE WRITING INSTRUMENTS

Just as we use pens, pencils and, in our electronic age, keyboards to write letters, various writing instruments are used for writing on the heart, including:

- Actions, our deeds both good and bad. The way we act and react toward others or the way people act or react toward us.
- Works, the service we do for or toward others.
- Words, this is one of the most powerful writing instruments of all. The words spoken to us can leave a deep message on our hearts. Proverbs 15:4 says, *"A wholesome tongue is a tree of life: but perverseness therein is a breach in the spirit."* And Proverbs 18:21 says, *"Death and life are in the power of the tongue . . . "* We write on the tablets of the heart with the words we use, and our own hearts have been written on with the words of others. Words like, "You're stupid! You're ugly! You're fat! You're worthless!" These words and those worse than these leave wounds when written on the heart. Words matter.

THE INK WE WRITE WITH

We all know that ink in an ink-pen leaves the impression on the paper from what we have written. We could say, "The ink leaves the mark." What is the ink that has left a mark on our hearts? Consider the following analogy:

Good ink leaves a good mark: Some people choose to write with good ink; good ink would include love, mercy, patience, compassion, hope, and encouragement. When we write on the hearts of people with good ink, then we leave good marks; we write a good message. We have all had people write on our heart with good ink, some of us have had more good ink written on our hearts than bad ink and some have had the opposite; more bad ink than good ink.

Bad ink leaves a bad mark: Some people choose to write with bad ink such as anger, resentment, bitterness, hate, fear, malice, destruction, and despair. All of us have had things written on our hearts with bad ink, and for those who have had more bad ink applied than good ink we know the pain the bad ink brings into our lives.

DOT YOUR I'S AND CROSS YOUR T'S

We have heard the expression that when writing we are to dot our I's and cross out T's, and when it comes to writing, this is really a small matter, but it is one of those things that distinguishes some of our letters. It is a small thing to dot an "I," but sometimes it is the small things that make the big difference. Even when it comes to us writing on someone's heart or someone writing on our heart, small things matter with matters of the heart.

CAN WE ERASE WHAT HAS BEEN WRITTEN ON THE HEART?

This is the big question! All of the destructive things that have been written on the heart, the words that have been written with the writing instruments of careless deeds, evil works, and hurtful words; can they be erased? I believe they can.

Jesus Christ wrote a new covenant. When a person believes in Jesus Christ as their Saviour, He washes all of the sin in their heart away, and if someone has written something on your heart that is painful, I believe you can ask Jesus to remove what is written and write something new in its place. Write this on your heart over something painful that might be there now. Jesus Christ loves you! You are very important to God! You can do great things! Your life matters! Your life has a special purpose!

If there is something painful written on your heart, I encourage you to forgive the one who wrote it and ask God to write something new in its place, open your heart up to Him, and ask Him to write on the tablet of your heart. Take time to read and meditate on the Bible and let Him write from its pages onto your heart. The painful, sorrowful things that are on your heart now can be erased with the love of God, and He can write new things. 2 Corinthians 5:17 says, *"Therefore if any man be in Christ, he is a new creature: old things are passed away; behold, all things are become new."*

PERSONAL REFLECTIONS

God has told us to pray and that gives us liberty to ask Him how to pray. God will show us the things written on our hearts that need to be removed. Ask God to give you wisdom and understanding to know what actions to take. Be prepared to deal with and take action in obedience where those things are concerned.

I will ask God to help me remove the following from my heart:

_____

_____

_____

_____

I would like the following to be written on my heart:

_____

_____

_____

_____

CHAPTER TWELVE
POUR OUT YOUR HEART

SOMETIMES WE MUST LET GO so we can gain, or we must release one thing, so we can take hold of something else. We must lay the old aside, so we can grasp the new. Where does all of this take place? I submit to you that it begins in the heart. Please carefully read the following Psalm of King David from Scripture. Psalm 62:5-8:

> *My soul, wait thou only upon God; for my expectation is from him. He only is my rock and my salvation: he is my defence; I shall not be moved. In God is my salvation and my glory: the rock of my strength, and my refuge, is in God. Trust in him at all times; ye people, <u>pour out your heart before him: God is a refuge for us. Selah.</u> (emphasis mine)*

This passage reminds us of how loving God is and how willing He is for us to pour the wounds of our heart out to Him.

David was familiar with having a broken heart. His own son Amnon committed rape. David's son Absalom turned against him and tried to divide his kingdom. David suffered other heartaches as well. We can gain strength from David's words.

Let's look at verse eight.

1. *"God is a refuge"*: David is encouraging us that we can trust God with everything, and that we can pour our heart out to Him. The word refuge means, "that which shelters or protects from danger, distress or calamity. A stronghold which protects by its strength, or a sanctuary which secures safety by its sacredness; and place

inaccessible to the enemy." As our refuge, we can go to God and know that He will protect what we tell Him and the secrets of our heart, which we share with Him, will be safe from the enemy.

2. *"Trust in Him at all times":* Trust can be a challenge for those who have been wounded, and trusting God is difficult for those who have been abused. But David invites us to trust God, encouraging us to trust God at all times. In the good times, in the bad times, in the up times, and in the low times, you can trust God when you stand to confront your giant, and you can trust Him in the darkest night. You can trust God with your most private secrets, and you can trust Him with your deepest wounds.

3. *"Ye people, pour out your heart before him, God is a refuge for us":* Here is the truth I want to encourage you with the most. Notice the words *"ye people."* That's us, you and me. God is a refuge for us. May I stress for you, you have a sanctuary! You have a God who loves you. You can pour your heart out to Him. You can reveal your heart to the One who has revealed His heart to you. God's heart is set on you with an unconditional and eternal love.

God knows our pain; He knows exactly where it hurts and why. He wants to help but can't as long as we silently hold that pain inside. Whenever you are ready to speak, God will be ready to hear, help and heal.

THE GREAT INVITATION

To empty yourself, to turn your soul up-side down in the presence of God, to pour your heart out to God, is to answer a great invitation. God invites us to come to Him. In Matthew 11:28-30 Jesus invites us, *"Come unto me, all ye that labour and are heavy laden, and I will give you rest. Take my yoke upon you, and learn of me; for I am meek and lowly in heart: and ye shall find rest unto your souls. For my yoke is easy, and my burden is light."* This is the great invitation offered to us. To bring our deepest wounds, the secret things we have never been able to share with anyone else, and the personal and private hurts that we have hid in the depths of our heart. Jesus Christ invites us to bring them to Him that He may bare them with us, and that He may give us rest in our soul.

Grief is a healing process, but people who never grieve will never heal as they should. To keep our grief and sorrow buried in our soul is distressing. But there is comfort and healing in trusting God in times of sorrow; there is hope in pouring our sorrow out before the weeping Christ.

POUR OUT YOUR HURTS TO THE HEALING SAVIOUR

A favorite passage of Scripture to me is Luke 4:18-19 where Jesus addresses a congregation of people in a synagogue at the very beginning of His earthly ministry with these words:

The Spirit of the Lord is upon me, because he hath anointed me to preach the gospel to the poor; he hath sent me to heal the brokenhearted, to preach deliverance to the captives, and recovering of sight to the blind, to set at liberty them that are bruised, To preach the acceptable year of the Lord.

Many times, in my life I have shared Jesus' words, *"he (God the Father) hath sent me to heal the brokenhearted,"* This is why Jesus Christ has made Himself available to you, so that you could go to Him with trust and pour your heart out to him. You can pour out your broken heart to the Healer of broken hearts.

Hurts that remain bottled up inside the soul will make you angry, bitter, and despondent. It is time to empty your heart of the hurts; it is time to trust God with the wounds, secret pain, and sorrow of the past. It is time to pour out your heart to a loving God.

ANSWER JESUS' INVITATION

We read in Matthew 11 that Jesus invites us to, *"Come unto me, all ye that labour and are heavy laden, and I will give you rest."* Will you take an opportunity to respond to this invitation? Go someplace where you can be alone with no interruptions or distractions. I encourage you to open your Bible to Matthew 11:28-30 and pray. Open your heart to the Heavenly Father, tell Him where it hurts, don't hold anything back, and pour out all the hurt, pain, anger, sorrow, and brokenness. Trust Him and pour out your heart before Him, *"God is a refuge for us..."*

IMAGINE THE LOVE JESUS CHRIST HAS FOR YOU!

As you are pouring your heart out through prayer to your loving Heavenly Father, take a moment, close your eyes, and imagine the Lord Jesus Christ standing there with His arms open to embrace you. Imagine the love that He has for you and how He is willing and ready to listen to every word you will speak to Him. Imagine the tears He has shed for you, and imagine Him wiping the very tears from your eyes and giving you the assurance that He loves you unconditionally, that He will never leave you or forsake you, that He has all power over the enemy, and that He will use His power of love to restore the teddy bear that has been taken from you. Find the courage now to take the initiative to pour out your heart to Him, grasp His outstretched hand, receive His loving embrace, and embrace Him with trust. Let Him place His loving and caring arms around you. He is listening . . . pour out your heart!

In my distress I cried unto the LORD, and he heard me.

Psalm 120:1

In the day when I cried thou answeredst me, and strengthenedst me with strength in my soul.

Psalm 138:3

PERSONAL REFLECTION

I will pour out my heart to God and tell Him:

_____

_____

_____

_____

CHAPTER THIRTEEN
HOPE

Which hope we have as an anchor of the soul, both sure and stedfast . . .
Hebrews 6:19

SOMEONE WISELY SAID, "HOPE IS faith holding out its hand in the dark." One of the greatest struggles for anyone who has been abused is that they can lose hope, and when hope is gone we stop believing that we can be victorious and that the future can be good. As I talk with and minister to people on an almost daily basis, it is my observation that a lot of people have given up hope. This book is not magical; I don't have the ability to take away all of your pain; I'm not humanly capable of erasing your past and replacing it with happy and wonderful events. I am unable to reconcile your relationships and mend your broken heart. But there is one thing I passionately believe I can try to do. I can tell you that there is hope! By taking the time to imagine the challenges you have faced, and the hurts you have experienced, I would like to encourage you, even implore you . . . there is hope! If you feel that you are about to give up, then I implore you . . . don't lose hope! And if you feel that you have lost hope, then I want to implore you to renew your hope!

HOPE DEFINED

The word hope is found one hundred and thirty times in the Bible, and it is defined as "a desire of good, a belief that it is attainable, confidence in a future event, to place confidence in; to trust in with confident expectation of good." With this definition in mind let's look into the Scriptures to find the "Hope of Hope"!

THE LORD GOD IS OUR HOPE

In Psalm 71:5 David says, *"For thou art my hope, O Lord GOD: thou art my trust . . . "* David's statement here reveals the mistake many people make is that they believe there is hope apart from the Lord God when the truth is that the only secure hope in this life and the life to come is in the Lord God. Hope is not in a form of government, hope is not in a program, hope is not in a philosophy, hope, real hope, a belief that good is attainable, confidence in a future event is secure in the creator of the universe, and the Lord God is the source of all hope!

PLOW IN HOPE

In 1 Corinthians 9:10 the Apostle Paul admonishes us, *" . . . he that ploweth should plow in hope; and that he that thresheth in hope should be partaker of his hope."* This is common sense advice for us to follow. Paul is using the familiar example of the farmer. The farmer plows his field to prepare it for sowing seed, and then he sows the seed with an expectation of a harvest. This analogy of the farmer may seem trivial but there is a great lesson here about hope. To plow is to labor, we also see the word thresheth (thrash), which means to beat out the grain from the husk. Simply put it means to separate what is usable from what is not usable. Now the important thing to remember here is that both of these activities, plowing and thrashing, amounts to a lot of hard work. But the farmer goes out into his field; he works hard to plow, to prepare the soil to receive the seed, then he plants the seed. He does all of this hard work with an expectation of eventually having a harvest, he "plows in hope"! He plows with an expectation of eventually having a harvest. Once he has the harvest brought in there is more work to do, and he must then separate the usable part of the grain from the part that is not usable. Sometimes what is not usable at first is later usable as seed.

Now here is where this idea of plowing in hope may be helpful. Getting to where you are right now emotionally and spiritually to where you can be is not only going to be a simple task, but is achievable, it can be done! You will need to be patient in your plowing, and you will need to plow (prepare) the soil of your heart. Then you will need to selectively sow seeds into your heart that will be pro-active and productive.

Some of the thrashing you will need to do is to evaluate the beliefs you have about yourself, about God and the Bible, and you will also need to evaluate the influences you have in your life. After you have evaluated these things you will need to do some "Threshing"! You will need to separate the wheat from the chaff (refuse, worthless material, fruitless). You need to separate those people from your life that drag you down, those that will not be helpful toward you producing the fruit you desire to produce. And you will need to separate the good beliefs from the negative and toxic beliefs.

"... *he that thresheth in hope should be partaker of his hope.*" We can never just wish for things to get better. The farmer does not wish for his field to be plowed and for the seed to be sown; he goes out and plows it himself; he labors in the field, plowing sowing, and then reaping. In order for you to get to the point of reaping in your life, you must begin to plow; you must put forth the effort toward doing what is necessary for your own healing and victory. You will partake of hope as you plow, sow, and nurture your life in hope.

God's eternal law of nature is still true, *"Be not deceived; God is not mocked: for whatsoever a man soweth, that shall he also reap"* (Galatians 6:7). Go forth and plow in Hope!

CHRIST IN YOU - THE HOPE OF GLORY

In Colossians 1:27 the Apostle Paul writes, *"To whom God would make known what is the riches of the glory of this mystery among the Gentiles; which is Christ in you, the hope of glory."* Jesus Christ is the source of all hope. By embracing Jesus Christ and placing our faith in Him as Saviour, He comes to abide in our soul. He which abides in you is hope. He is the expectation of Good! Therefore, you have within you an eternal hope!

Does that mean that everything will come easy for you? Does that mean that it will be easy to let go of the past and embrace the future? Does that mean you will not have challenges and bad days? No, but with Christ in you, it does mean there is hope! It does mean you can plow and expect a good fruit to follow. It means that you are not alone and that you have not been forsaken, and it means you don't have to confront the past alone. You don't have to confront the future alone either.

A LIVING HOPE

We find these words in 1 Peter 1:3 *"Blessed be the God and Father of our Lord Jesus Christ, which according to his abundant mercy hath begotten us again unto a lively hope by the resurrection of Jesus Christ from the dead,"* Our hope in Christ is an active, vivacious, vigorous, strong, and energetic hope! The hope that is in Christ is a hope that does not fade away. Certainly, we will get discouraged, and we will become weary. But when we renew our hope that is in Christ, we will find that His hope will still be there for us. His is a hope that exist because He is the resurrected Saviour, He never grows weary, and He never loses faith in us! HE LIVES and because He Lives, Hope Lives, and You too can live! Live and love again!

OUR HOPE IS AN ANCHOR FOR OUR SOUL

Hebrews 6 has some other wonderful truths about hope that will be a blessing and encouragement to your soul.

Verse 11: *"And we desire that every one of you do shew the same diligence to the full assurance of hope unto the end."* My desire and prayer for you is that you be diligent, don't give up, keep moving forward, keep working toward healing, and be assured of a brighter future in the days to come.

Verse 18: *"That by two immutable things, in which it was impossible for God to lie, we might have a strong consolation, who have fled for refuge to lay hold upon the hope set before us:"* We can take comfort in knowing that God does not change, and God does not lie. When we have those bad days, those old memories and emotions make their way into our thoughts; we can go to our Heavenly Father for shelter, protection, and assurance that He is still there, and hope is still set before us.

Verses 19-20: *"Which hope we have as an anchor of the soul, both sure and stedfast, and which entereth into that within the veil; Whither the forerunner is for us entered, even Jesus, made an high priest for ever after the order of Melchisedec."* The word anchor here is used symbolically and means something that gives us stability or security that which we can depend upon. Again, I remind us from verse eighteen that because God does not change, and God cannot lie, we have a hope that is secure and stable.

The statement *"... which entereth into that within the veil;"* is a special blessing, and I would like to take more time to elaborate than I can here. However, the meaning connects with the statement in verse eighteen which also refers to having a refuge. We can enter into the veil; that is, we can enter into the very presence of God. This is possible because the Lord Jesus Christ is there serving as our High Priest, He understands every emotion and struggle we have ever experienced, and because He died and rose again and now sets in the presence of God, He has made our hope sure and stable. Living Hope!

PERSONAL REFLECTIONS

Who in my life diminishes my hope and is toxic to me?

_____
_____
_____
_____

What do I need to do about this?

_____
_____
_____
_____

What or who have I falsely placed hope in?

_____
_____
_____
_____

In these areas of my life I will continue to plow in hope, realizing that my healing requires that I not give up and work toward healing and victory:

_____

_____

_____

_____

CHAPTER FOURTEEN
PERSONAL PEACE

These things I have spoken unto you, that in me ye might have peace . . .
—John 16:33

IT HAS SEEMINGLY BECOME A joke in our society that when you ask people what they want in life they respond, "World Peace!" This answer is given in a rather sarcastic way because we know that World Peace is not a realistic ideal. The good news is the Bible tells us World Peace will come when Jesus Christ, the Prince of Peace, returns. On the other hand, in our hearts we all have a strong desire for personal peace.

For those who have experienced abuse, personal peace seems too unrealistic to even consider. When someone has lived in years of turmoil, peace is uncomfortable. It is a foreign concept because bad things have happened to you for so long that you are not sure how to respond when peace is experienced. There is that constant worry that everything is going too well and you're just waiting for the ball to drop.

On the other hand, some people are so used to having personal peace that they don't acknowledge it or appreciate it until it is no longer there. So, when peace is obtained, value it. And I assure you, personal peace is possible! Let's look at the possibility of personal peace and what having it would mean in everyday life. We begin by defining what peace is.

PEACE DEFINED

Peace: freedom from agitation or disturbance by the passions, as from fear, terror, anger, anxiety or the like; quietness of mind; tranquility; calmness; quiet of conscience.

Peace is the absence of turmoil. Think of peace this way. Silence is not the presence of something; silence is the absence of noise. Darkness is the absence of light, and peace is the absence of turmoil or trouble in our lives. Does that mean to have peace in our lives that we never have any problems at all? No, but it does mean that even when there is a storm on the sea of life we can have peace in the boat we are sailing in.

The reality is there is tribulation in the world, and we can't change that; however, we can be at peace in a troubled world. Notice these powerful words of Jesus from John 16:33, *These things I have spoken unto you, that in me ye might have peace. In the world ye shall have tribulation: but be of good cheer; I have overcome the world.* The Lord Jesus tells us here that in Him we *"might"* have peace. The word *"might"* has a double meaning, which clearly explains what Jesus is telling us. *"Might"* means it is possible to have personal peace and that the power to have peace is available to us through Him. He also makes it clear that *"... in the world ye shall have tribulation,"* you are already keenly aware of this fact; you have experienced tribulation; it is peace that you desire now. So, in acknowledging that we will have tribulation in the world Jesus tells us, *"... be of good cheer; I have overcome the world."* Peace is possible in the midst of the turmoil and troubles of this world because Jesus Christ has overcome this world.

TESTIMONIES ABOUT PEACE

I asked some friends to share with me their testimony of what Personal Peace means to them, this is what they said: "I think personal peace is obtained when we surrender to Christ. I think it is extremely important; however, you have to surrender to it daily. I make a daily decision to allow God's perfect peace to carry me. Some days it is an hourly decision. Satan likes to use our past hurts to constantly attack us. I have learned I must memorize scripture and use scripture to ward off the bad and sad thoughts." Another said, "We can choose peace rather than give way to fear and worry. Inner personal peace resulting from a relationship with God allows us to keep things in proper perspective. It's like we can go through difficult things because in Him we know where our home is. Being abused and living through it and to come out on the other side with peace in my heart is all because I now know that Jesus Christ is my source of personal peace."

HIS NAME IS PEACE

There are several names given to God the Father and His only begotten Son Jesus Christ such as "Elohim," which means Strong One, "Jehovah Jireh," which means The God who provides, "Jehovah Rophe," which means The God who heals and the name we want to focus our thoughts on, and "Jehovah Shalom," which means The God of Peace. We find this in Judges 6:24 *"Then Gideon built an altar there unto the LORD, and called it Jehovah-shalom (the God of Peace)."*

In Isaiah 9:6, we have the prophecy of the birth of Jesus Christ, and we find the names He would be given, *"For unto us a child is born, unto us a son is given: and the government shall be upon his shoulder: and his name shall be called Wonderful, Counsellor, The mighty God, The everlasting Father, The Prince of Peace."* His name is *"Prince of Peace"*; the word name as we are using it here signifies His title, His attributes, His will, and His purpose. Peace is part of the character of God, and His desire is that you to experience His peace by seeing Him as the source of personal peace. Meditate on this truth for just a moment; Jesus Christ is the Prince of Peace. That means that Jesus Christ possesses the power of peace; He is the sovereign ruler of peace, and in Him we can find personal peace.

WHAT CAN BE DONE TO KNOW PERSONAL PEACE?

For someone who has experienced tribulation, what can be done to know peace? From the Scriptures let's consider the following truths:

JESUS CHRIST HAS OVERCOME THE WORLD.

"... be of good cheer; I have overcome the world." I find that the Bible always has the perfect solution and always provides me with understanding about

everything in life, just as it says it will. Notice the statement, *"... be of good cheer."* The word cheer means to dispel gloom and sorrow. On the Cross, the Lord Jesus Christ confronted every evil power and every evil action that would ever exist. He literally looked Satan in the eye and took him on face to face. Jesus Christ shed His blood on the Cross and gave His very life for our personal peace. Three days later, He rose again sealing the victory for everyone that would believe in Him. He overcame the World and the evil one that currently manipulates people in this world. Jesus Christ made it possible for us to dispel gloom and sorrow and to be of good cheer.

THE LORD JESUS CHRIST TOLD US THINGS THAT GRANT US ASSURANCE OF PERSONAL PEACE.

"These things have I spoken unto you, that in me ye might have peace." We could have a detailed lesson based on that statement; however, we won't take the time to do that now. So, allow me to outline what Jesus spoke to the disciples in this conversation that begins in John 13 that will help us know personal peace.

1. Jesus washed the disciple's feet (John 13:2-10).

   In this humble act, Jesus expressed His own humility and His servant attitude toward us. There is personal peace in knowing that the Lord is willing to serve our needs, and that He is willing to perform the most menial task to assure us of comfort and peace.

2. He told of His own Betrayal (John 13:21).

   There is personal peace in knowing that the Lord Jesus Christ understands our experience of having been betrayed. He was betrayed by someone that was close to Him and by someone you would not have thought would hurt Him. Yet Jesus called him friend.

3. He told Simon Peter that he would deny Him (John 13:36-38). There is personal peace in knowing that the Lord Jesus confronted the one that had wronged him, even if He did so before the act of denial was committed. He also Prayed for Simon Peter and forgave

him for the hurt that He caused. Because of Jesus Christ, we have peace in knowing that we can confront those we need to confront, we can pray for those who have hurt us, and we can forgive them!

4. Jesus told us a bright future is ahead (John 14:1-3). John 14:3 says, *And if I go and prepare a place for you, I will come again, and receive you unto myself; that where I am, there ye may be also.* There is personal peace in knowing Jesus Christ as a personal Saviour. Although this world is in turmoil, we have the assurance from Jesus Himself that one day He will come for us and take us to where He is, and we know that in His presence there is perfect peace.

5. Jesus Told us that He is the way, truth and life. In John 14:6, Jesus said, *I am the way, the truth, and the life: no man cometh unto the Father, but by me.* My friend Matt Hackney made this observation after going through a time of turmoil in his own life, "Peace isn't feeling; it's knowing. It isn't a place, it's a person. It isn't chance; it's a choice." Jesus Christ is the what to peace, He is the truth of peace, and He is the life of Peace.

6. Jesus told us we could tell Him (John 14:13-14). He said we could ask anything in His name. There is personal peace in knowing that we can go to Him through prayer and tell Him absolutely anything.

7. Jesus told us He would send a comforter. The words of Jesus in John 14:16-18 are so precious, *And I will pray the Father, and he shall give you another Comforter, that he may abide with you for ever; Even the Spirit of truth; whom the world cannot receive, because it seeth him not, neither knoweth him: but ye know him; for he dwelleth with you, and shall be in you.*

I will not leave you comfortless: I will come to you. The word comforter means one who will come alongside to help. The Holy Spirit is the comforter that Jesus has sent to every believer. There is personal peace in learning that we can go to Him, we can listen to Him as He communes with our spirit, and He will speak comfort to us.

8. Jesus told us He would give us peace. In John 14:27, Jesus said, *Peace I leave with you, my peace I give unto you: not as the world giveth, give I unto you. Let not your heart be troubled, neither let it be afraid.* Notice the statement, *"my peace I give unto you";* not what we think peace is, not what the world defines as peace. But Jesus Christ offers us the peace which is His. The peace of knowing He loves us unconditionally. He can deliver peace to us because He received the punishment for our sin; He is able to forgive us of all our sin and bestow us with His peace. The peace is in Him because, on the Cross, He confronted every evil action that could ever be brought against us. Philippians 4:6-7 says, *Be careful for nothing; but in every thing by prayer and supplication with thanksgiving let your requests be made known unto God. And the peace of God, which passeth all understanding, shall keep your hearts and minds through Christ Jesus.* There is peace in knowing that we can impart to Him all of our burdens, hurts, wounds, and pain through prayer. And His peace cannot be explained, but it can be known, and His peace will keep (guard, protect) our hearts and minds.

PEACE OF MIND

Thou wilt keep him in perfect peace, whose mind is stayed on thee: because he trusteth in thee.

Isaiah 26:3

And the peace of God, which passeth all understanding, shall keep your hearts and minds through Christ Jesus. Finally, brethren, whatsoever things are true, whatsoever things are honest, whatsoever things are just, whatsoever things are pure, whatsoever things are lovely, whatsoever things are of good report; if there be any virtue, and if there be any praise, think on these things. Those things, which ye have both learned, and received, and heard, and seen in me, do: and the God of peace shall be with you.

Philippians 4:7-9

The old saying "The idle mind is the devils workshop" is true today. Satan will put thoughts in your mind, bring back old memories, and do all he can to place turmoil in your thoughts. It is important that we train our minds and discipline ourselves to keep our minds on thoughts that are true, honest, just, pure, lovely, of good report, of virtue, and praise.

Keeping your mind focused on the truth and promises of God, feeding our mind with the Word of God, listening to good music, reading good books, and having good conversations will help you keep your thoughts on peaceful things. It is just as important to avoid the old memories and sometimes to do so we must also avoid certain people that like to talk about the "good ole days" that weren't so good.

This is a continuous battle, you must determine to take control of your own thoughts and focus on the love, strength, mercy, and the grace of God. I suggest that you write some Bible verses on a sheet of paper and keep it with you at all times; anytime your mind begins to wander to things that take your peace from you read those verses to help you rein your thoughts back where they should be. Psalm 119:165 says, *Great peace have they which love thy law: and nothing shall offend them.* Memorize Bible verses that will help you keep your thoughts on God's peace. Philippians 4:7-9 is a good place to start.

Jesus said, *"In the world ye shall have tribulation . . . "* In this world we will have challenges, and you will have bad times. Even when things go bad, your Prince of Peace, the Lord Jesus Christ will be there to guide you to the right path. You have to embrace peace as you have embraced Jesus' counsel. Don't push that feeling of relief away when it is within your reach. Thank the Lord Jesus Christ for the personal peace that is available to you! You can have personal peace!

Mercy unto you, and peace, and love, be multiplied.

Jude 1:2

PERSONAL REFLECTIONS

My definition of "Personal Peace":

_____

_____

_____

_____

The way I see Jesus Christ as my source of Peace:

_____

_____

_____

_____

I know Jesus understands my hurts because:

_____

_____

_____

_____

I realize that in the world I will have tribulations because:

_____

_____

_____

_____

Steps I will take toward having "Personal Peace":

_____

_____

_____

_____

CHAPTER FIFTEEN

BEAUTY FOR ASHES

To appoint unto them that mourn in Zion, to give unto them beauty for ashes, the oil of joy for mourning (sorrow), the garment of praise for the spirit of heaviness; that they might be called trees of righteousness, the planting of the LORD, that he might be glorified. And they shall build the old wastes, they shall raise up the former desolations (things destroyed), and they shall repair the waste cities, the desolations of many generations.

Isaiah 61:3-4

ASHES . . . IN over thirty years of ministry I have witnessed scores of people come to Jesus Christ with ashes; that was all that was left of their lives after Satan had his way. I have seen God take those ashes and exchange them with beauty. I witnessed God take the oil of mourning and put joy in the heart of the grieved. And I have witnessed God take heaviness from a broken heart to see that mended heart give praise to God. I have witnessed people who have been beaten down and had all but given up, rise up, and become tress of righteousness for the glory of God. What I'm saying to you is that you can rise up; the former desolations can be raised up. You can live and love again.

My desire now is to equip you, so you can move forward from here. Hold your teddy bear firmly in your arms rise up and move forward. The actions I am about to suggest to you come from my thirty plus years of witnessing God work in people's lives and from suggestions submitted by the team of people who have helped me with this book. Here is what one of our team members shared from their heart:

"For me, I found a good church and eventually found an older lady that showed me I could trust her, and I confided in her about many of the things that had happened in my life. I worked closely with her to learn Scripture and to learn about what real love should be.

"I would suggest finding a good Christian mentor, that one person (a lady for women or a man for men) that has earned your trust and respect. Pray and ask the Lord to lead you to someone; work with that person starting slowly. Learn scripture, work a Bible study together, and then enter into a 'need to work through some stuff' relationship with them. Ask them to keep your conversations confidential and ask them to pray for guidance as you work together. Chances are they or someone close to them has had these experiences themselves.

"It is very important to learn scripture as you go. The Bible will become your stones and slingshot for battling your giants.

"In depth details are not as important as just working through the emotional wounds. Pray, pray, and pray some more as you walk your journey to living and loving again. Learn to live a new life in Christ; He has suffered for you and with you; He has not hurt you. Jesus Christ is your best friend; He will love you forever, no matter what! He walks the journey before you, making a way for you!

"I personally pray for each person this book will touch. I know the journey is hard, scary, and emotionally tough, but I believe God has great plans for you, so I am praying for you."

—Melissa Davis

"This journey is a process. The big step for me was to understand my self-value; I still struggle with that at times. When one discovers who they are in Jesus Christ, the value that He sees in them, they will see value in themselves. No matter how abused and beat down you have been you must learn that you have value. You have to see that there is hope, set one small goal at a time so you can keep moving forward. It is important to find a good church that will love you and encourage you. Keep praying and encouraging friends close to you. Read your Bible and talk to God because He will be your best friend. Memorize and meditate on Bible verses that will keep your mind and heart focused on what is important. Know and believe that you are not alone, and that people do care."

—JLH

EVALUATE WHERE YOU ARE

Back before we had GPS devices, we use to use maps to travel with. I can remember getting lost on several occasions while I was traveling somewhere. I knew where I was going, but at that moment I wasn't sure where I was. I would stop at a roadside gas station or store and ask someone where I was, then I would look at my map, determine where I was, look at where I was going, and then I could move forward. In the process of taking back your teddy bear, you must evaluate where you are emotionally, relationally, and spiritually. Is there anyone I need to forgive? How do I view myself? What wounds do I need to address spiritually? What do I need to do to embark on the path of healing and victory? This is where a good Bible pastor or spiritual mentor is important; ask them to help you assess where you are on your journey in comparison to where you are going and which road you should be on now. This is also something to pray about; ask God where you are in this journey and which road to be on and remember the Bible is the best compass.

YOUR NEXT STEP

The next decision you make toward healing and victory, the next thing you choose to believe about your journey, about taking back your teddy bear, and the situation at hand is crucial. You have choices to make; you can choose now to become bitter or to become better. You can choose to stay down and defeated, or you can choose to rise up with Jesus Christ and live a new life in Him. You can choose to live and love again, or you can choose to do nothing.

TAKE ACTION NOW

Don't wait, begin to apply the biblical principles you have learned in this book. Review the chapters that have especially helped you; read and re-read them if it helps. Learn the Bible verses that have helped you and act on them now!

DRAW CLOSE TO GOD

The most important relationship you have is the one you have with Jesus Christ; draw near to Him. Talk to Him through prayer, listen to Him by reading the Bible, and fellowship with Him by getting acquainted with other Christian people. Learn all you can about Jesus Christ: who He is, what He has done for you, and how much He loves you. Read through the book of John in the Bible. John provides a wonderful and warm perspective of Jesus Christ, and you will receive a clear picture of Jesus and His love for you!

FEED YOURSELF SPIRITUALLY

Reading from the Bible every day is the best resource of all, but another good resource is a devotional to read from every day; there are some good ones available. I like devotionals that come with a journal. Ask your pastor to recommend one for you. Learn to meditate on Bible truths, feed your soul with good Christian music, and read books that will strengthen your soul and spirit.

FIND A CHURCH TO CALL HOME

A good Christ centered local church is the best support group you can have in your life. Find a church that is Bible focused and has a heart for people. Pray and ask the Lord to lead you to the one He wants you in. Attend every service you can and let your soul and spirit be strengthened by good Bible teaching and preaching.

FIND A SPIRITUAL MENTOR

Melissa mentioned this in her letter and how much it helped her. If you already have a good church home go to your pastor, ask if he could help direct you to someone that could disciple you with your circumstances. This person is crucial in your life, they must believe the Bible, and they must have a biblical view of life in order to help you effectively.

WRITE A LETTER

Some people find it helpful to write a letter to their abuser. My suggestion concerning this is to take your time in writing the letter, write it from your heart and pray about it carefully. You may want to discuss the letters content with your spiritual mentor. The purpose of the letter is to share with your abuser how you feel, what you have struggled with and how you are letting go of the hurts and pressing on with your life. I suggest that you express to them that you will no longer allow them to have control over your thoughts, your emotions or your life. Let them know you are dethroning them from any influence or control over you. Then tell them that you forgive them because God has given you the ability to do so. This part is very important: Don't write your letter until you know in your heart that you have truly forgiven them. Also, this may be a letter you deliver to your abuser or just keep in a safe place. For some abuse victims it brings more hurt to deliver the letter, but often writing such a letter has a healing and "letting go" affect. In most cases it is helpful to write the letter even if the abuser is deceased.

JESUS CHRIST UNDERSTANDS AND RELATES TO YOU

No matter what today is like and no matter what you may face tomorrow, on the good days, the bad days, and the in between days, always remember that Jesus Christ understands what you are dealing with. He cares about you and your struggles, and He is always just a prayer away. Isaiah 53:3-5 says this about Jesus:

> *He is despised and rejected of men; a man of sorrows, and acquainted with grief: and we hid as it were our faces from him; he was despised, and we esteemed him not. Surely he hath borne our griefs, and carried our sorrows: yet we did esteem him stricken, smitten of God, and afflicted. But he was wounded for our transgressions; he was bruised for our iniquities: the chastisement of our peace was upon him; and with his stripes we are healed.*

MAKE LIFESTYLE CHANGES

To overcome the past, we must sometimes change what we are doing in the present. Change in your life begins in your heart with what you believe about God, His Bible, and yourself. To live victoriously over the past, you must let go of the past, the events of the past, and even some people in your past. Then you must embrace the present and the future. *Restored* is about practicing the Bible principles of faith, forgiveness, restoration, prayer, worship, and a NEW LIFE in Jesus Christ. I repeat a verse used other times in this book. In John 10:10 Jesus said, *"The thief cometh not, but for to steal, and to kill, and to destroy: I am come that they might have life, and that they might have it more abundantly."* It is not easy, but you can live and love again!

WHO YOU ARE

Everything that has happened in your life is part of who you are, but it does not define you. We don't always choose our circumstances, but we always choose what we do about them. The past does not define you, those who have hurt you do not define you, and your circumstances do not define who you are. Your relationship with God, the faith in your heart, the dreams and goals you have for yourself, what you desire to do to help others, and the difference you want to make in your own life and in the lives of those you love, these are the things that define who you are!

LIVE

Throughout this book I have referenced John 10:10 where Jesus said, *I am come that they might have life, and that they might have it more abundantly.* From Jesus' words, I want to encourage you to live that life. Live the life of freedom from bondage of the past, live the life that is in Jesus Christ, the life of peace, hope, love, and victory. This does not mean that everything is going to be perfect in your life. We live in a struggling world, and we will always have challenges, but we can rise up. Living the abundant life will require faith, putting forth your best effort every day, and staying close to people who will help you and love you. Keep your thoughts and heart focused on your relationship with Jesus Christ and the goals you have for your life. If you have breath, then you have life, and if you have life, there is hope. Go forth and live!

GIVE BACK

As you grow as a person and become stronger spiritually, you will become an inspiration to others. And you will find opportunities to encourage others; use this opportunity to give back. Mentor and disciple people who are struggling with the same challenges you have struggled with. In order to do this effectively, you must be strong yourself; you can only life others up so long as you have the strength to do so. But once you have that strength use it, lift others up and you will find it to be very fulfilling.

A LETTER TO MY READERS

Dear friend,

I realize we have not covered everything, I'm sure there are specific things in your situation that I'm unaware of and unable to address. My prayer for you is that something shared here in this book has helped you heal, helped you believe that you do have value, and that you can live victoriously. I pray that you rise up and be a tree of righteousness, the planting of the Lord that He might be glorified. Go take back your teddy bear and your life, "beauty for ashes" and live and love again!

In God's Love,

Dr. Don Woodard

Isaiah 61:3

TESTIMONIES

TESTIMONY OF GRACE

I am Melissa Davis, servant of God, wife to one amazing husband and father, mom to eleven, and grandmother to two that I am also raising. God has blessed me far beyond my wildest imagination.

The beginning of my life was filled with feelings of being unwanted, unloved, and abandoned. At ten months of age, my birth father was gone, and my birth mother left me on a neighbor's door step and walked away. Child Protective Services picked me up and went to another residence where my brother was left, and we were taken in by my grandmother and grandfather.

While my grandmother worked, my aunt would babysit us and then one day she told my grandmother that she couldn't keep us part time any longer; she wanted to be our mom. My grandmother agreed, and thus we became my aunt and uncle's children. We were raised under their last name and never knew anything different until around the age of ten when my cousin got angry and told me I was never wanted and that my real mother threw me away and my parents that raised me felt sorry for me, so they gave us a home. Raised by parents who were active in both the church and the Christian school we attended made life seem two sided. On one side we were the perfect loving church family, on the other side we were lied to and unwanted, thrown away rejects that were taken in due to pity.

By the age of eleven, I was angry, I felt unloved, unwanted, and not worth the skin I was in. I began looking at every blonde-haired lady wondering if she was the mom that threw me away. Did I look like her? I looked at every man and wondered if he might be my real father. Did I look more like him? Did I get the true story? Was I really thrown out like the garbage?

It didn't help that at this age my grandfather began doing things to me that I hated, but he also would say things like "this is why you're here," "they know what we do," and "if you ever tell they won't believe you" among many other things. Within a year, he would hold knives to me and threaten to kill my mom or my grandmother if I told anyone. This went on for many years.

By the age of 12, I had found my birth certificate and knew my birth parent's names and to my wonderment found that the man I thought was my uncle who was always in trouble, in jail, or who knew where, was my birth father.

My teen years were plagued by many angry evil acts. I would try telling friends what was happening, but they only gave me things to "help me not feel it." The guys would tell me this would help me not feel anything or this would make my grandfather stop. That was my beginning into the drug world.

Between 12 and 17, not only was my one grandfather abusing me, but my other grandfather had, and he got caught but nothing more than angry words was the result. My brother and my cousin both "practiced," and one of my uncles just "wanted to see if I was ready for boys."

I married the day after turning 17 in hopes that I could escape this world of being unloved and used up. My oldest son came, yet the abuse continued and my then husband began getting paid to drop me off and let me "work" for my grandfather at the tool shack. This became my husband's income.

Finally, at the age of 19, I was able to tell my mother what had been happening and the anger and hatred felt like my fault because I didn't tell her before. By 21, my grandfather had tried again to abuse me, and I put him in jail. Since I never told anyone about the abuse before I turned 19, he only spent three days in jail and was released. No one believed me. Drugs, alcohol, and suicide attempts were constants in my life over the next 8 years.

In October 1995, I wanted to die more than ever before. I had failed to protect my baby and she was hurt in unspeakable ways. I blamed myself for her birth father's actions. Child Protective Services got involved, and I had to choose to fight or die. I wanted to die, but somehow, I decided to fight. Through intense Christian counseling, I began to learn that I might be worth something if to no one else but to my kids. I started going to church. I started hearing how God truly loved me and had plans for my life. I learned how God used the Woman at the well to change an entire City and how Paul, who was once Saul, was forgiven for murdering Christians, yet God changed him, and he became greatest minister of his time. I thought if God could use a murderer and a woman like that back then and if God never changed, then maybe just maybe He could change me and use my life for His glory.

It would take another seven years before I realized I was not saved. I tried to work my way to God, go to church, be really good, everything I could think of to do what was right I tried; when I failed, I failed horribly and would battle depression and then try to climb my way back up to Gods good graces. There would be many ups and downs before I would find the love of Jesus Christ at the age of 30 years old.

At 30 years of age in October 2002, I found a loving Christ who gave me a new heart and made me feel true love for the first time since I was a young girl still innocent. I felt wonderful relief and God began to change me from the inside out.

By the time I married my husband, I could not have any more children, so I was a ready-made family with three children and many scars from the past that I so badly wanted to heal from. My husband would teach me that the past was behind me, and I just needed to focus on Christ today and for the remaining future. We married in February of 2004.

By October 6, 2006, we would begin the path to becoming foster parents, and in November 2006, we received our first placement. We fostered for three years and chose to close our home by adopting the 8 children in our home. This would finish our family of eleven children.

There have been so many blessings over these past twelve years. Together with our two grandchildren in our home we have twelve children at home, and we all love and serve God together in our local church here in our home town. We are blessed to have my parents living next door to us to help us if and when we need help with our children. My parents also love and serve God in the church I grew up in at Palmer, Texas.

Over the past 12 years, we have seen God bless us beyond measure. We have children whom have lived the life of foster care and adoption and are serving the Lord in every way possible. We have a church family that is so supportive and loving that even includes my special needs children. God blessed me with the co-writing of a book, my Associate of Science Degree in Biblical Counseling, the recording of three CDs, speaking/singing engagements, and many more opportunities to share His Love and Salvation.

Through the power of our loving Lord Jesus Christ, we will continue to move forward wherever He wants us to serve. We will continue to serve Christ together. I will continue to speak and/or sing and share His love and healing to all that will listen. I want others to know that we cannot work our way to heaven. Only the acceptance of Gods free grace and love by faith in His son Jesus Christ can we ever enter the Kingdom of Heaven.

Melissa Davis,

Child of God

FROM NOBODY TO SOMEBODY

Growing up, I was the fourth out of five kids. I always felt that I got lost in the shuffle of the family. I was shy, quiet, and tried to please everyone, which only hurt me in the long run. Sometimes it's best if you speak up and voice what's going on within you. If you don't, no one will know to help if needed.

Here's some of my story . . .

Being a tomboy, I never felt I fit in with the girls. I was the girl out with the guys playing basketball, football, baseball, or whatever they were doing I was in on it. While the girls stood in groups talking, boring! I was different, and my escape was on the basketball court. I went to a Christian school; I would play basketball after school. When it was time to go home, I ran upstairs to buy a soda. The machine didn't work . . . the custodian came around the corner, an older man . . . he told me he could help me. He told me to follow him into this room, so I did. As I walked into the room he shut the door, locked it, and pushed himself onto me. My mind was racing; I had no idea what was happening to me. He told me not to tell. I felt so dirty, so ashamed, felt so worthless. I didn't fit in, now for sure I was different. Yet, I never talked about it to anyone. My shame, my secret.

After that took place, I felt alone and sadly that was not the first time something like that took place. I began to wonder why God bothered to create me in the first place. What was I here for, to be hurt and abused by men? So fast forwarding to my dating life, I met the man of my dreams, or so I thought. He was wonderful, smart, had beautiful eyes, to me in my eyes he did no wrong. Until the day I found a porn magazine in his brief case. I was crushed. I brought it up to him, and he promised no more, but that was a lie because I found more. Porn is a problem that can't just be shut off without help. The more one is into porn the more things within that person changes. After that I began to see other things. My world began to fall apart.

We were married for 25 years and have two wonderful boys. See, my husband always loved other women. He treated me like I was a nobody; I was stupid; I could do no right, ever; I could never be what he was wanting, and nobody can compete with a man who is filled with porn in his mind. It took me years to realize that. I always thought I was the problem, but in reality, the problem is with him.

As my boys were younger, all my focus went onto them. I was part of the PTA I worked in the schools; I coached basketball, soccer, softball, and volleyball after school. I tried to keep busy, so my mind wouldn't run on the problems. Night was the worst when my mind would run wild; I would lie in bed, husband next to me and silently cry myself to sleep. No one cared, as my mind always told me. To me if the man I married couldn't love me, nobody would. I became hopeless.

I grew up in church; I knew God loved me in my heart, but my head told me other things. Like, why am I here? Why did God even create me? To be abused by men physically, mentally, and sexually? Was that why I was here? I fell into depression thinking I was alone. No one cared. That was all a lie because God always loved me. I was letting the devil steal my joy and rob me of any hope.

It took me years, five years after my divorce to seek help. It took years of family and friends praying for me to get me to the place for me to be able to seek help. All the stuff that happened to me was pushed under the rug; it was my secret and shame to hide because, to me, somehow, I asked for it, somehow it was my fault, so talking to someone about it would only bring more hurt and shame on me. So, I kept quiet about my pain and just tried to smile. I had little to no hope; I just went through the motions day by day. I went to work, went to church but just went through the motions.

There is hope in Jesus. I found a great counselor, a man of God who is there to help and encourage people. We've talked a lot, really, he did the talking, and I listened a lot. I had to go back to God. He was always there and always a part of my life, but I had to get back to a relationship with Him. I've learned to pray a lot more, meditate a lot on God's word. Today when my mind runs wild with bad memories from the past, I have to go back to God and what has helped me heal, praying a lot, and meditating on positive aspects of life like the peace of God. It's a process; it won't happen overnight, healing takes time. Healing can happen, hope can happen and will happen, but we have to seek help. God is there to help us, always. He loves us, always. Knowing Him means we are never alone. He is our hope. Just go to Him with it all; He wants you to have peace. Seek help, go to God, and meditate on the goodness of God. It will bring hope to you like it has to me.

Somebody God Loves,

J. H.

Indiana

REDEEMED

Believing I am in control of my own life and what situations I allow myself to remain in has been the first step in recovering from abuse and a toxic lifestyle. As part of the abuse cycle, I was programed to think that this is it, this is my life. How can I ever escape this? I believe God allowed me to come across the precise information I needed to begin my ability to question if this were true. I came across an ad online for domestic violence help. It didn't happen overnight, but as God plants a seed it soon blossoms to glorify him. That small five seconds I took to view a pop up ad online began my escape.

Once I got into shelter he didn't stop there, no, God doesn't leave us in the middle of what He starts; He always see's us through. I immediately met a Christian woman and began to go to church. The first few times I went I felt so dirty as if I wasn't a good enough person to attend church because of my past. That's the second thing God revealed to me, this was exactly where I needed to be, and so I eventually felt led to hit my knees at the altar. My soul cried out to him, "Please Lord, help me! I have made such a mess of my life, and I haven't the strength to go on. I cannot do it on my own." I put my faith in God that day.

Slowly, my life became easier and my children and I were beginning to feel the normalcy of an abuse free life. I made mistakes along the way, but God never gave up on me. He has taught me lessons over the years, some of which made me feel my prayers were unheard. Looking back now I see God's hand closing doors and leading me to a life I never believed I could achieve. I didn't believe in myself, but He believed in me. The devil is a liar and he will seek you out at your darkest times and appear to you as beautiful as the forbidden tree Eve was so curious to eat from. But remember you belong to Jesus, so the devil can only destroy you if you allow him to.

I learned to surround myself with other Christians; they made me feel safe, and I rarely left the church. I volunteered at a mission where my children's grandfather preached. I was feeding the hungry and homeless because it made me feel close to the Lord. I learned along my way that He is always near, but it did comfort me at the time to stay shut away from the evil world outside.

I have remained single now for going on seven years because I am afraid of whom I might end up with. Abusers are never apparent monsters in the beginning so it's not easy to know what you've gotten mixed up with until you're in a prison once again. I know this is something God is teaching me slowly because that is the pace I need to begin trusting again. He began by teaching me I could trust in Him and now I have a church family I trust. My heart needs to take baby steps, and He allows me time to heal.

I have always loved music and so during my journey I have come across lyrics that have spoken to my heart and soul, and I cannot hear them without the spirit of the Lord falling upon me and tears streaming down my cheeks. I cry when I feel his presence but not out of sadness but absolute purity of love, trust, and this bond I feel to my Saviour. I actually became wonderful friends with a woman who serves in the music ministry at her church (God continuously leads me to people who aid in mending my broken heart and she has been one of them). She took me to my first Christian concert. There were two songs played that left me lingering in the sweet spirit of Jesus and those two songs have been my go to when I need to draw close to him and remember I am not the person I used to be, I am no longer in danger living in fear for my life, I am safe, I am loved, I am a precious jewel to him, I am capable of more than I give myself credit for, I am worthy, and I need not fear tomorrow because no matter what it brings He will bring me through it.

You must understand that this life is temporary, our souls are eternal. You have a soul that is hungry for God! He is real, and He will supply you with something you don't even know you're missing. Reach out to Him and let Him take over. Feel the peace of his embrace and a love that you can't imagine. He has healed me in so many ways, and I want what I have experienced for every person out there, especially the broken hearted who are imprisoned by abuse. I lean on the words of Proverbs 3:5-6 which says, *"Trust in the LORD with all thine heart; and lean not unto thine own understanding. In all thy ways acknowledge him, and he shall direct thy paths."*

The Bible, prayer, and some very special Christian songs are my special "go to's" that drawl me nearer to the Lord and keep me focused on my life as it is now and as I continue to grow. If you search Him out, He will reveal Himself to you in ways that touch your heart in only a way that He can. Building a relationship with Jesus Christ is not like any other relationship, He has never left me alone, ashamed or angry. He will change your heart, soften you, and tear down that wall you have instinctively put up to prevent being hurt.

So often we begin as compassionate, big hearted, and naïve young women, eager to fulfill our dreams, find our soul mates, and live happily ever after. Nobody tells us what we are to do when we find ourselves taking wrong turns leading us to broken homes, abuse, alcohol, drugs, being single mothers living in poverty and taking up with men who aren't our prince charming's but do supply a roof over our heads and food in our children's bellies. I believe these abusive men seek out broken women and that is how they lure us in. They provide us with a home and tell us they want to save us, and we feel like we need to be saved.

A man is never going to be our Saviour. What we are searching for is the Lord, but if nobody tells you, how do you know? It is not like me to be single for almost seven years; I was as co-dependent as they come. But let me tell you the truth. Since I have rebuilt my life myself on my own without a man, I have value for this life, and I no longer will let just anyone in. I have worked so hard... Yes, God didn't make it easy for me to get myself together, and I put forth the effort, but I can see now it was to build value to this life I have today. There were times I didn't think I could make it. I cried a lot of tears, dragged my babies out of bed in all kinds of weather sometimes at 4am, I have gone without sleep, I have stood in the line at social services asking for financial help, I have juggled childcare issues and being a mom when I had to also put school work first, I have gone to college classes and taken finals sick with high fevers, but I didn't give up. I took it one day at a time and when it got too much to handle, then I turned it all over to God, and He carried me through.

On May 13, 2016, I graduated college with an Associate of Science degree in nursing. I have a great job as the Registered Nurse Unit Manager at a health and rehab facility near my home. My two children and I live in a beautiful apartment that is safe and very comfortable for us. I don't look back as much as I use to, I keep looking forward as I count the blessings I have in my life today. Do you think it was possible for a drug addicted, homeless, single mother, traumatized by years of abuse to achieve this on her own? I know there is no way I did this on my own... it all began with that seed God planted that blossomed into my great escape. If I can overcome my toxic life so can you, with God leading you.

Suzi F.

I am Redeemed

Proverbs 3:5-6

Virginia

LARGER THAN LIFE

I grew up thinking I knew how to live life to the fullest. I thought what could be better than throwing caution to the wind by partying, getting high, and getting completely wasted at the age of thirteen? I had a long road ahead that pointed straight to how very wrong I was. After years of substance abuse and running from the trauma of being sexually abused at the age of six by a fourteen-year-old neighbor boy, I realized it was time to face the past that had shaped my future into something I never considered possible. As a young adult I became a Christian and my relationship with Jesus Christ made it possible for me to overcome the substance abuse and trauma of being sexually abused as a child; yet there remained other giants to confront in my life. Because of my choices as a teenager, I found myself living larger than life in so many ways. At my heaviest, I weighed 680 pounds. My continuous struggles have brought me to a place of a new view on life. Now, 110 pounds lighter and 65 inches thinner, I'm taking back my life from the jaws of obesity.

There are things about myself that will always be larger than life; the hopes and dreams of my heart are to use my life now to make a positive difference in the lives of others. I know now that it is possible to face any challenge in your journey of life, and you too can take your life back and live larger than life.

Sean Mulroney

President of Teens of America, radio show host, and bestselling author

TeensofAmerica.net

A LETTER FOR FORGIVENESS

When my mother was 8 years old she was violated by her grandfather in the most awful way. This was not revealed to me until I was in college. Growing up in a home with a mother who had been abused was not always easy. I always knew something was not right. My mom was at times very bitter and angry. My mom would take this bitterness and anger out on my father and at times my brothers and me. I knew my mom loved us, but living with her was like walking on egg shells at times.

My first Christmas home from Bible College my mom had one of her explosive episodes, and she felt ashamed and embarrassed. I went back to college and on summer break my family came and picked me up from school. On the ride home, my mom told me that she was sorry and that she was getting Christian counseling for some issues she has. She did not go in to detail, but I told her that I was happy for the help she was receiving.

One night when I was home, I was looking for something in one of the dressers and found a workbook that dealt with sexual abuse. That night I asked my mom about the situation and what she told me made my heart sink. She told me that her grandfather, who I never knew, had sexually violated her when she was eight years old. She explained to me that this is why she battled such bitterness, anger, and hurt for so long. I began to put the puzzle pieces together. She would lash out at my father and take her hurt out on him and us because of the pain she was experiencing inside.

Her Christian counselor told my mom that one of the steps she would need to take was to forgive her grandfather. The counselor challenged my mom to write a letter explaining her feelings and forgiveness to her grandfather who was not living, but to write it as though he could see and hear it. My mom was very honest and transparent in the letter and was able through the help of God to forgive her grandfather. It was liberating for my mom to let out this secret hurt and helped her to begin the process of healing and forgiving. I am thankful that Dr. Woodard was led by God to write this book. I know this book will help many who have gone through the pain that my mom has experienced. Thank you.

God bless you,

D. D. Jr.

LIVING AND POWERFUL WORDS

THE BIBLE IS FILLED WITH words of hope, strength, power, peace, healing, and much more. We have compiled select Scripture for you as a resource and reference for you to refer to when you struggle in your journey, and we also encourage you to read and study the Bible daily as it will give your strength and understanding.

> For the word of God is quick, and powerful, and sharper than any twoedged sword, piercing even to the dividing asunder of soul and spirit, and of the joints and marrow, and is a discerner of the thoughts and intents of the heart.
>
> Hebrews 4:12

TRUST

The God of my rock; in him will I trust: he is my shield, and the horn of my salvation, my high tower, and my refuge, my Saviour; thou savest me from violence.

2 Samuel 22:3

As for God, his way is perfect; the word of the LORD is tried: he is a buckler to all them that trust in him.

2 Samuel 22:31

Though he slay me, yet will I trust in him: but I will maintain mine own ways before him.

Job 13:15

But let all those that put their trust in thee rejoice: let them ever shout for joy, because thou defendest them: let them also that love thy name be joyful in thee.

Psalm 5:11

O LORD my God, in thee do I put my trust: save me from all them that persecute me, and deliver me.

Psalm 7:1

How excellent is thy lovingkindness, O God! therefore the children of men put their trust under the shadow of thy wings.

Psalm 36:7

What time I am afraid, I will trust in thee.

Psalm 56:3

Trust in the LORD with all thine heart; and lean not unto thine own understanding. In all thy ways acknowledge him, and he shall direct thy paths.

Proverbs 3:5-6

Behold, God is my salvation; I will trust, and not be afraid: for the LORD JEHOVAH is my strength and my song; he also is become my salvation.

Isaiah 12:2

As soon as Jesus heard the word that was spoken, he saith unto the ruler of the synagogue, Be not afraid, only believe.

Mark 5:36

Jesus saith unto her, Said I not unto thee, that, if thou wouldest believe, thou shouldest see the glory of God?

John 11:40

But these are written, that ye might believe that Jesus is the Christ, the Son of God; and that believing ye might have life through his name.

John 20:31

HOPE

He giveth power to the faint; and to them that have no might he increaseth strength.

Isaiah 40:29

Fear thou not; for I am with thee: be not dismayed; for I am thy God: I will strengthen thee; yea, I will help thee; yea, I will uphold thee with the right hand of my righteousness.

Isaiah 41:10

The LORD also will be a refuge for the oppressed, a refuge in times of trouble. And they that know thy name will put their trust in thee: for thou, LORD, hast not forsaken them that seek thee.

Psalm 9:9-10

When my father and my mother forsake me, then the LORD will take me up.

Psalm 27:10

Be of good courage, and he shall strengthen your heart, all ye that hope in the LORD.

Psalm 31:24

Cast thy burden upon the LORD, and he shall sustain thee: he shall never suffer the righteous to be moved.

Psalm 55:22

For thou art my hope, O Lord GOD: thou art my trust from my youth.

Psalm 71:5

Thou art my hiding place and my shield: I hope in thy word.

Psalm 119:114

I wait for the LORD, my soul doth wait, and in his word do I hope.

Psalm 130:5

By whom also we have access by faith into this grace wherein we stand, and rejoice in hope of the glory of God.

Romans 5:2

Rejoicing in hope; patient in tribulation; continuing instant in prayer.

Romans 12:12

Now the God of hope fill you with all joy and peace in believing, that ye may abound in hope, through the power of the Holy Ghost.

Romans 15:13

And now abideth faith, hope, charity, these three; but the greatest of these is charity.

1 Corinthians 13:13

That by two immutable things, in which it was impossible for God to lie, we might have a strong consolation, who have fled for refuge to lay hold upon the hope set before us: Which hope we have as an anchor of the soul, both sure and stedfast, and which entereth into that within the veil.

Hebrews 6:18-19

Blessed be the God and Father of our Lord Jesus Christ, which according to his abundant mercy hath begotten us again unto a lively hope by the resurrection of Jesus Christ from the dead.

1 Peter 1:3

STRENGTH

The LORD is my light and my salvation; whom shall I fear? the LORD is the strength of my life; of whom shall I be afraid?

Psalm 27:1

The LORD will give strength unto his people; the LORD will bless his people with peace.

Psalm 29:11

Thou art my hiding place; thou shalt preserve me from trouble; thou shalt compass me about with songs of deliverance. Selah.

Psalm 32:7

But the salvation of the righteous is of the LORD: he is their strength in the time of trouble. And the LORD shall help them, and deliver them: he shall deliver them from the wicked, and save them, because they trust in him.

Psalm 37:39-40

He giveth power to the faint; and to them that have no might he increaseth strength. Even the youths shall faint and be weary, and the young men shall utterly fall: But they that wait upon the LORD shall renew their strength; they shall mount up with wings as eagles; they shall run, and not be weary; and they shall walk, and not faint.

Isaiah 40:39-31

Fear thou not; for I am with thee: be not dismayed; for I am thy God: I will strengthen thee; yea, I will help thee; yea, I will uphold thee with the right hand of my righteousness.

Isaiah 41:10

And he said unto me, My grace is sufficient for thee: for my strength is made perfect in weakness. Most gladly therefore will I rather glory in my infirmities, that the power of Christ may rest upon me.

2 Corinthians 12:9

I can do all things through Christ which strengtheneth me.

Philippians 4:13

For God hath not given us the spirit of fear; but of power, and of love, and of a sound mind.

2 Timothy 1:7

PEACE

I will both lay me down in peace, and sleep: for thou, LORD, only makest me dwell in safety.

Psalm 4:8

Great peace have they which love thy law: and nothing shall offend them.

Psalm 119:165

Thou wilt keep him in perfect peace, whose mind is stayed on thee: because he trusteth in thee.

> Isaiah 26:3

For I know the thoughts that I think toward you, saith the LORD, thoughts of peace, and not of evil, to give you an expected end.

> Jeremiah 29:11

And he said unto her, Daughter, be of good comfort: thy faith hath made thee whole; go in peace.

> Luke 8:48

Peace I leave with you, my peace I give unto you: not as the world giveth, give I unto you. Let not your heart be troubled, neither let it be afraid.

> John 14:27

These things I have spoken unto you, that in me ye might have peace. In the world ye shall have tribulation: but be of good cheer; I have overcome the world.

> John 16:33

Therefore being justified by faith, we have peace with God through our Lord Jesus Christ.

> Romans 5:1

Let us therefore follow after the things which make for peace, and things wherewith one may edify another.

> Romans 14:19

Now the God of hope fill you with all joy and peace in believing, that ye may abound in hope, through the power of the Holy Ghost.

Romans 15:13

Be careful for nothing; but in every thing by prayer and supplication with thanksgiving let your requests be made known unto God. And the peace of God, which passeth all understanding, shall keep your hearts and minds through Christ Jesus. Finally, brethren, whatsoever things are true, whatsoever things are honest, whatsoever things are just, whatsoever things are pure, whatsoever things are lovely, whatsoever things are of good report; if there be any virtue, and if there be any praise, think on these things. Those things, which ye have both learned, and received, and heard, and seen in me, do: and the God of peace shall be with you.

Philippians 4:7-9

Now the Lord of peace himself give you peace always by all means. The Lord be with you all.

2 Thessalonians 3:16

Mercy unto you, and peace, and love, be multiplied.

Jude 1:2

FORGIVENESS

And forgive us our debts, as we forgive our debtors.

Matthew 6:12

And when ye stand praying, forgive, if ye have ought against any: that your Father also which is in heaven may forgive you your trespasses.

Mark 11:25

And forgive us our sins; for we also forgive every one that is indebted to us. And lead us not into temptation; but deliver us from evil.

Luke 11:4

Take heed to yourselves: If thy brother trespass against thee, rebuke him; and if he repent, forgive him. And if he trespass against thee seven times in a day, and seven times in a day turn again to thee, saying, I repent; thou shalt forgive him.

Luke 17:3-4

Then said Jesus, Father, forgive them; for they know not what they do. And they parted his raiment, and cast lots.

Luke 23:34

Saying, Blessed are they whose iniquities are forgiven, and whose sins are covered.

Romans 4:7

And grieve not the holy Spirit of God, whereby ye are sealed unto the day of redemption. Let all bitterness, and wrath, and anger, and clamour, and evil speaking, be put away from you, with all malice: And be ye kind one to another, tenderhearted, forgiving one another, even as God for Christ's sake hath forgiven you.

Ephesians 4:30-32

If we confess our sins, he is faithful and just to forgive us our sins, and to cleanse us from all unrighteousness.

1 John 1:9

RENEWED HEART / RENEWED LIFE

Purge me with hyssop, and I shall be clean: wash me, and I shall be whiter than snow. Make me to hear joy and gladness; that the bones which thou hast broken may rejoice. Hide thy face from my sins, and blot out all mine iniquities. Create in me a clean heart, O God; and renew a right spirit within me. Cast me not away from thy presence; and take not thy holy spirit from me. Restore unto me the joy of thy salvation; and uphold me with thy free spirit.

Psalm 51:7-12

A new heart also will I give you, and a new spirit will I put within you: and I will take away the stony heart out of your flesh, and I will give you an heart of flesh.

Ezekiel 36:26

For which cause we faint not; but though our outward man perish, yet the inward man is renewed day by day.

2 Corinthians 4:16

Therefore if any man be in Christ, he is a new creature: old things are passed away; behold, all things are become new.

2 Corinthians 5:17

ABOUT THE AUTHOR

Dr. Don Woodard has served in the ministry for over thirty years; serving as a pastor, evangelist, author, and Biblical counselor. He and his wife Debbie live in Troutville, Virginia, and they have five children and currently seven grandchildren. Dr. Woodard serves as senior pastor of Beacon Baptist Church in Salem, Virginia. He frequently speaks in conferences and has appeared on television and radio to address teen suicide, teen drug addiction, teen violence, sexual and emotional abuse, and family challenges in America. He also serves as an advisor to ministries for addiction and homes for troubled young people.

For more information about
Dr. Don Woodard
&
Restored: Living and Loving After Abuse

please contact:
www.facebook.com/
Restored-Living-and-Loving-After-Abuse-210835189440015
PO Box 490
Troutville, VA 24175

For more information about
AMBASSADOR INTERNATIONAL
please visit:

www.ambassador-international.com
@AmbassadorIntl
www.facebook.com/AmbassadorIntl

RU is a faith-based recovery program designed to help those with stubborn habits and addictions.

FIND A LOCAL CHAPTER NEAR YOU

EXPERIENCE OUR RESIDENTIAL PROGRAM IN ROCKFORD, IL.

FIND MANY RESOURCES ONLINE YOU CAN USE AT HOME

BREAK THE CHAINS OF ADDICTION

RU Recovery is a transforming addiction recovery program developed from over two decades of experience working with thousands of addicts worldwide. If you have tried everything else, and are looking for something that "just works" then this program is for you.

INFO@REFORMU.COM | 815.986.0460
RURECOVERY.COM